BUT MOM, I DON'T WANT TO MOVE!

BUT MOM, I DON'T WANT TO MOVE!

Easing the Impact of Moving on Your Children

Susan Miller

TYNDALE

Tyndale House Publishers, Inc.
Wheaton, Illinois

ISBN: 1-58997-166-3

A Focus on the Family book published by
Tyndale House Publishers, Wheaton, Illinois

Unless identified otherwise, Scripture quotations are taken from the New American Standard Bible®. Copyright © the Lockman Foundation 1960, 1962, 1963, 1968, 1971, 1972, 1973, 1975, 1977, 1995. Used by permission. (www.Lockman.org). Scripture quotations marked (NIV) are taken from the Holy Bible, New International Version®. NIV®. Copyright © 1973, 1978, 1984 by International Bible Society. Used by permission of Zondervan Publishing House. All rights reserved. Scripture quotations marked (KJV) are taken from the King James Version.

Focus on the Family books are available at special quantity discounts when purchased in bulk by corporations, organizations, churches, or groups. For more information, contact: Focus on the Family, 8605 Explorer Drive, Colorado Springs, CO 80920; or phone (800) 932-9123.

Library of Congress Cataloging-in-Publication Data

Miller, Susan, 1956-
    But mom, I don't want to move! : easing the impact of moving on your children / Susan Miller.
        p. cm.
    Includes bibliographical references.
    ISBN 1-58997-166-3
    1. Moving, Household. 2. Moving, Household--Religious aspects--Christianity. I. Title.
    TX307.M55 2004
    648'.9—dc22

                                                                                    2004002881

Editor: Kathy Davis
Cover Design: Amy Kiechlin and Joy Olson
Cover Photo: Mark Waters

Printed in the United States of America
1 2 3 4 5 6 7 8 9 10 / 10 09 08 07 06 05 04

To the moms
who are the nurturers and caretakers of the family
during the transition of moving.

And to Bill Jr. and Ginger.
I love you with all my heart!
Your biggest fan,

Mom

~

Contents

Foreword

The news comes in. It's official: You're going to move.

Now you've got to go in and talk to the kids. In particular, you've got to talk to that one child who has already exhibited all the warmth of barbed wire when it comes to even entertaining the thought of moving.

But Mom, I Don't Want to Move!

I love Susan Miller's title because it hits so close to home for so many of us. Susan knows from firsthand experience the challenges of making more than a dozen family moves. She knows that while packing and picking a new place to live are stressful, getting the kids to pull together can be far more draining.

For many parents, trying to get a child on board with a move—and helping him or her positively adjust after the move—is like trying to push a long rope. You push to the right, the rope bends to the left. You push to the left, the rope bends to the right.

How do you get leverage in your child's life to make the very best of a move? The answer to that question, I strongly believe, is in the book you hold in your hands. For what Susan Miller does in an exceptional way is help you face the emotions and gain the insights you need to make the best move possible. You *can* get a rope to go in the direction you want it to go, but you only do so by holding on to one end of the rope while walking in a positive direction. Let Susan guide you in the steps you need to take to get things moving and make the very best out of a challenging situation—before, during, and after your move.

On a personal note, I've known Susan and her husband, Bill, for over a decade. I've seen her bless and build up and encourage women, first at our home church, and now across our country. I feel she is without peer, and the "go to" person on making successful, God-honoring moves.

You're going to love this book, but even more, I urge you to get involved in Susan's N.E.W. Ministries. This is a support system for moms just like you who are facing, or have just made, a move. You don't have to do it all alone. There are N.E.W. Ministries classes across the country as well as great resources—like this book—that can speak words of encouragement, hope, and wisdom into your life.

May the Lord bless your move, your life, your family, and especially give you the wisdom to love and lead that child who says, "But Mom, I don't want to move!"

JOHN TRENT, PH.D.
President, StrongFamilies.com
Scottsdale, Arizona

Acknowledgments

To those who lived it . . . all the moms and kids who wrote letters, gave interviews, and sent in surveys from all over the nation. Your experiences and stories of pain and joy, struggles and triumphs, bring real life to the pages of this book. Thank you for ministering to other movers by sharing your heart.

Thank you to my Focus Family:

Larry Weeden, who always encouraged me to write another book;

Mark Maddox, for catching the vision for this book;

Clark Miller, who understands the need to minister to women who move;

Kathy Davis, my editor, for your professional skills, mixed with warmth and care, during the editing process. You were a delight to work with;

Phil Hildebrand, Stacey Herebic, and Lance Roth in Licensing and Trade Marketing;

Kurt Birky's creative team: Joy Olson, Mark Boswell, and Amy Kiechlin, for pulling it all together and taking it to the finish line!

Thank you to my N.E.W. Ministries family:

Joan Langston, words cannot convey how grateful I am that you have stood beside me in this ministry all these years. I couldn't do it without you. You are the best!

Sharon Nowlin and JoAnn Smith, loyal ministry staff, your commitment to the day-to-day ministry operations allowed me the freedom to spend the time necessary to write;

Lisa Watson and Mary Milt Ford, whose experienced eyes carefully proofed my manuscript before it went to Focus on the Family;

Ann Klinkenbeard, who spent hours compiling research material;

MaryAnn Szymanski, who organized a prayer team of 125 women across the nation to pray for this book project during the months of writing;

The prayer team, whose faithful prayers and words of encouragement refreshed my spirit each day;

The "Dream Team," a group of 25 women who have experienced moving and now serve in N.E.W. Ministries. Your wisdom and insight about the needs of moving moms were invaluable in writing this book.

And, I am grateful to:

Bev Lehsten, who encouraged me with God's Word and biblical principles all along the way;

Nancy Del Duca, who always holds my hand and lifts my heart as I write;

Bill Jr. and Ginger, whose stories, experiences, and emotions through our moves have given me sensitivity to kids who move and the insight for this book;

My husband, Bill, whose unconditional love and care for me has filled the chapters of my life. Your wise counsel guided me through this book. You listened and encouraged as I labored over each word. Once again, God has used you in my life to complete His work.

My Lord and Savior, who filled my heart and mind with His words. He is the Author and Finisher of this book.

Introduction

Dear Moving Friend,

I knew in my heart that writing this book was eventually going to happen. Over the years, I have listened to the cry of your heart. As a parent, you desperately want to help your children in their transition and adjustment of moving. In some way, you want to protect them from going through the very things you have experienced in moving: your fear of leaving behind all that is familiar to face the unfamiliar; your pain when you have to say good-bye to close friends, family, and community; your overwhelming feeling of loneliness and loss of identity as you move to a new place. In other words, you want to prepare them as best you can with ways to cope and adjust and handle the many changes that moving brings. For some of you, it takes all your energy just to deal with your own emotions that are raw and confusing.

I know what you are thinking and feeling at this very moment, whether you are getting ready to move, or if you have recently moved. After uprooting 14 times since I've been married, 10 of those times with children, I've been where you are mentally and emotionally in the maze of moving. I have been angry, depressed, sad, and just plain weird sometimes. I've felt happy and excited about going somewhere new and different. I have cried bucketsful of tears and grieved over all the losses that come with moving. I have laughed at the silliest things in order to keep a perspective on all the change and chaos around me. I've blamed God and praised God for circumstances beyond my control.

It all started when my husband, Bill, chose a career in hotel/restaurant management. Climbing the corporate ladder meant moving every two to three years. For many years we relocated within the southern states. Then came a company transfer to the Wild West! With the move from Atlanta, Georgia, to Phoenix, Arizona, came the most difficult transition and adjustment I had ever encountered. It was a change point emotionally and spiritually in my life that soon evolved into a passion to encourage other women in their journey of moving.

That passion eventually became the stepping-stone for starting Newcomers Enfolding Welcoming (N.E.W.) Ministries. This ministry now reaches women all over the world who move, and impacts them with the love, hope, and encouragement of Jesus Christ. God also used that move as a catalyst for me to write the book *After the Boxes Are Unpacked: Moving On After Moving In.* It is based on my moving experiences, coupled with the biblical principles I know and trust. It was written especially for you, from my heart.

I never cease to be amazed at how God took the moves in my life and used them all for His glory. And I know He wants me to travel with you one more time down the road of moving. This time it will be to encourage and equip you, as you in turn encourage and equip your children through their journey of moving. Believe me, I've made my share of mistakes in parenting each time we uprooted our children to move. I didn't always do the right thing or say the right thing, and I wasn't always there for them emotionally. I can, however, share with you what I have learned along the way, and even what I would have done differently.

I want you to hear more than just my voice, so N.E.W. Ministries sent a national survey to parents, teachers, and counselors asking for their input on how to help children in the transition and adjustment of moving. You'll get their perspective as well. More importantly, you'll hear from children and teens as they share their heart about moving. More than 10 million children ages 1 to 14 and over two million teenagers ages 15 to 19 relocate each year, and they have significant input on the subject![1]

At the end of each chapter you'll find questions that you can discuss together as a family, with your child individually, or use as personal reflection. Hopefully this will promote open communication with one another and a clearer understanding of each other's feelings and emotions. It will also present the opportunity for vulnerable sharing to take place and God's Word to encourage each of you. Included is a chapter on how to pray for your children with prayers for specific needs.

My purpose in writing this book is twofold. It will equip you to help your children and teens before, during, and after a move. It will include practical tips, stories from those who have been down the same road, and lots of encouragement along the way. However, it's not only about knowing what to do; it's also about what God will teach you through the process and the experience. Biblical principles and Scripture will be your road map. By knowing, trusting, and living out the biblical principles of an immovable God, you will have a profound effect on the life of your child. And in the process, God will change *you*.

Never lose heart and never give up! (Galatians 6:9) This book will not only equip you, but will give you the hope and encouragement you are looking for. I'm standing on the sidelines cheering you on!

FROM MY HEART,
SUSAN MILLER

PART I

Before the Move . . .

"Do We Have to Go?"

CHAPTER ONE

Preparing the Rooms of Your Heart for a Move: First Things First!

I was so wrapped up with my own feelings, as well as the details and planning of the move, that I felt like I wasn't there to listen and talk to my children. I wish I had been there more for them.

MARY, A MOVING MOM

"I am emotionally and physically exhausted," said Chris with tears in her eyes. Her three children were in school, and she had come by to tell me they were moving in three weeks. "I feel like I'm being pulled in a hundred directions, and there is nothing left in me to help my children through this move. Where do I begin?" she said in desperation. As I sat and listened to her all-too-familiar story, my heart ached for her. I could see the anguish in her eyes and sensed her feelings of helplessness. I couldn't fix things or change her circumstances, but I could give her encouragement and comfort to help ease the pain. Somehow just being together seemed enough for her at the time.

Her words *Where do I begin?* have often come to mind. I thought of the familiar instructions heard so many times on an airplane: "In case of an emergency, secure your oxygen mask first, then help your child!" Before you can begin to help your child through the transition and adjustment of moving, you need to take a deep breath and take care of yourself. So many times during the moving process I would run on empty, with nothing left over to fill our children's needs. This brings me to the question, "How are you doing?"

Keep in mind that moving is much like an emotional roller-coaster ride. One minute you're going up, the next minute you're going down, and you're never quite sure what the next curve will bring. Right now you may be hanging on to the roller coaster of moving, not sure how you are going to land. Have you even stopped for a minute to check your emotions about this move? Before we begin to focus on your children, let's take some time together just for you. I want to go beyond your smile. After 14 moves, I know so well how a smile can cover a multitude of feelings. I want to go straight to your heart.

Preparing Your Heart

Picture your heart as a home with many rooms. You prepare the rooms of your home for moving out and for moving in. Have you prepared the rooms of your heart for this move? Perhaps you have closed off a room that holds the sadness of leaving behind beloved friends and family. Maybe there is a room of fear for what the future holds, and that fear is keeping peace from your heart. There could be a room of chaos filled with to-do lists, or a room of exhaustion that prevents joy from entering in.

It doesn't matter how much information you have on preparing your children for their move. If you haven't taken the time to prepare your heart emotionally and spiritually, you will be like an empty vessel unable to pour out the love, care, nurturing, and encouragement your children need during this time.

Where do you begin? Here are 10 steps to prepare your heart for a smooth move. The first four steps are the foundation for all the rooms in your heart.

Step 1: Remember Who Accompanies You

The most important thing for you to remember in your transition is that you are not going through it alone. It's very easy to slip into a pattern of thinking you're carrying this overwhelming responsibility all by yourself! If you are a single mom moving, you might feel especially alone. Even though I was married, at times I felt very much alone in the moving process. Yet God assures us that His presence goes with and even ahead of us. He will never leave us, fail us, or forsake us. Even now when I feel alone and overwhelmed, I am reassured through God's Word that He is with me! You can prepare a room in your heart with this scripture: "The LORD is the one who goes ahead of you; He will be with you. He will not fail you or forsake you. Do not fear or be dismayed" (Deuteronomy 31:8).

Step 2: Recall God's Faithfulness

Oh, how easily we forget! I can become so consumed in seeing only what's happening around me right now and how it's not going according to the "plan of Susan" that I quickly forget God's faithful track record with me in the past. He has always met all my needs, although not necessarily all my wants (Philippians 4:19). It is all according to His plan, not mine!

I remember one time when we were making two house payments because our house in Atlanta had not sold before we moved to Phoenix. I could not understand why we had to endure such a financial hardship. After one year, the Atlanta house finally sold. Somehow God faithfully provided a way financially for us to make it month by month. I learned some faith-building lessons that year in trust, patience, and God's provision. Prepare a room in your heart with faith, not sight (2 Corinthians 5:7).

Step 3: Count Your Blessings

Regardless of your circumstances, I know you can find the blessings in your life. Put aside all the "what ifs" and the "if onlys" and start counting. Instead of having a pity party, have a praise party!

On one of our moves during early marriage days, we lived in an apartment complex that was still under construction. Each day all I saw was the dirt and mud that surrounded us. Every time someone came inside they tracked in more mud. There wasn't anything that wasn't covered with dust inside. My "if only" list grew and spilled over into a bad attitude and a grand pity party.

Then one day as I looked out the window, my eyes shifted from the ground to the sky. The sun was gleaming through the trees, and the sky was bright blue. I caught a glimpse of a bird high on a treetop, singing his heart out. Suddenly I realized how I had been looking down and seeing only the negative circumstances. What I needed to do, instead, was simply "look up" to see the positive. I slowly began to count my blessings in spite of the mud, dirt, and dust.

Try looking up instead of down. It's amazing what you'll see. Changing your focus can make all the difference in the world. Wallpaper a room in your heart with Psalm 118:24 (NIV): "This is the day the LORD has made; let us rejoice and be glad in it."

Step 4: Stay Grounded in What's Important

A lot of things are going on in your life right now. To-do lists are getting longer, as well as all the suggestions on what to do and how to do it. You are probably being pulled in a lot of directions and feel some-what scattered. As I have said many times in the upheaval of moving, "I'm bouncing off the walls. Watch out!" Sometimes I need to be pulled back to the center and get my feet back on the ground before I can move forward.

Are you listening to the voice of the world telling you all the things you have to do and say? Are you listening to society telling you how to look and act to make this a smooth and easy transition in your life? Try listening to the voice of God as He tells you to follow His direction and listen to His wisdom. God's to-do list is short, just "Come, follow me" (Matthew 19:21, NIV). He also says, "Abide in Me" (John 15:4) and everything else will fall in place. Prepare a room in your heart with God's Word to keep you rooted and grounded in His love (Ephesians 3:17).

Step 5: Stop and Smell the Flowers

In other words, take time to be good to yourself! Schedule some self-care by taking a break to rest your body, renew your mind, and restore your spirit. Whether it's before or after your move, the whole transition is hectic and exhausting. Emotions are high and nerves are on edge. You will need an extra measure of energy in the days ahead, so I am giving you permission for a little Rest, Renewal, and Restoration (R, R & R). Some of you won't slow down otherwise! Because I care about you . . .

Get a good night's sleep. You don't have to stay up all night cleaning out drawers or straightening up the house for the movers to come. True confession: I've done it! I even had a moving friend who dusted every-thing before her move!

A 10- or 15-minute nap would always restore me. Love those naps!

Take a walk—a long walk. It will help to clear out the cobwebs in your mind.

Enjoy silence by turning off the television. It will help to settle your thoughts.

Eat right even if you are on the run. This is not the time to eat junk food and skip meals.

When all else fails, turn to comfort foods. We all have our favorites. Mine is peach ice cream!

Take your vitamins and drink lots of water. (Do I sound like your mother?)

Do some light reading with a good book or a magazine.

Listen to soothing music on a CD or cassette.

Pamper yourself and have your toenails painted a pretty color.

Sing your favorite song and maybe do a little dance along with it.

You might want to start journaling your thoughts and feelings about this move. Add some personal prayers. It will be good to look back and see how God has answered them.

Make the time to read your Bible. It will renew your mind with God's truth at a time when things may seem confusing. He will speak to your situation through His Word. One verse can change the course of your day and your life.

Prepare a room in your heart just for yourself!

Step 6: Ask for Help from Your Friends

I was always so hesitant to ask anybody to help me when we were in the moving process. I didn't want to impose or inconvenience anyone. Oh, how I could have used an extra pair of hands, a listening ear, or lunch shared over a cardboard box.

Over the years I've learned that by not asking for help, I was denying my friends the blessing of being a part of the process of our leaving.

Don't be afraid to ask for help. Part of saying good-bye can be expressed through the gift of serving. The time spent together is priceless. The memories will be cherished. You will be doing them a favor by picking up the phone and saying, "I need you." Prepare a room in your heart for a friend to come and "bear one another's burdens" (Galatians 6:2).

Step 7: Be Prepared for the Blues Clues

Recognize the clues when you get the blues! You may feel sad about leaving a great job, dear friends, or a home that's become a part of you. You could be feeling depressed and overwhelmed about uprooting and starting all over again. You might be angry at your husband or even his company for a move you didn't want to make. The fear of going to a new place, not knowing if you will like it there or whether you will fit in, may loom in the back of your mind. Anxiety about choosing the right house, school, community, church, doctor, and even a hairdresser could keep your thoughts preoccupied.

My dear moving friend, you are so normal! With over 40 million people relocating each year, you can count on the kaleidoscope of feelings shared by others like you. When your life becomes unraveled from

Five things you can do in five minutes for a quick refresher

- Put on some lipstick.
- Stop and sit down.
- Make a cup of tea.
- Walk outside and take a deep breath.
- Say a prayer for five things you are thankful for.

a move, you are going to have a flood of emotions and feelings. As the tapestry of your life is woven together again, it is my prayer that it will be with threads of peace, contentment, and joy. "The LORD bless you, and keep you; the LORD make His face shine on you, and be gracious to you; the LORD lift up His countenance on you, and give you peace" (Numbers 6:24-26). Prepare a room in your heart where you can acknowledge your feelings and seek God's peace.

Step 8: It's Okay to Cry If You Want To

Moving is change. With change comes loss. With loss comes grieving. With grieving come tears. When you move, grieving is a natural progression of what happens when you lose someone or something that is a meaningful part of your life. The loss of your friends, community, home, job, and even your church family can fill you with grief even before your move takes place.

Marlena stopped by our office to say good-bye before she moved to Japan. "I'm sorry," she said. "Every time I talk about moving, I can't seem to stop crying." Even though she was looking forward to this move, she was grieving over the loss of dear friends and moving so far away. Saying good-bye was bittersweet for her.

Kendra, whose husband found a new job in Kansas, said to me, "I should be so happy because this is a great move for my husband's career and I'll be closer to my family, but I can't stop crying." She had put down roots in the community and church for the short time they were there. Having to uproot and transplant so soon was not easy.

For both of them, the inescapable grieving had begun. The release valve was tears. I comforted each friend as I shared in her loss and held her as we cried together.

Prepare a room in your heart for tears to flow. It's okay to cry. "After you have suffered for a little while, the God of all grace, who called you to His eternal glory in Christ, will Himself perfect, confirm, strengthen and establish you" (1 Peter 5:10).

Step 9: When the Heat Is Up, Stay Cool

There will be times when the stress is rising and the pressure is on. Nothing will go according to plan: You are late for a farewell get-together; you can't find the house documents you put in a safe place; the people who might buy your house are coming back and bringing their relatives; and the school just called for you to come and get your sick child. Sound familiar? At times like this, keeping a sense of humor and being flexible are your only chances for survival. Humor can release stress and help put chaos in perspective. Being flexible with a to-do list or a tight schedule can help ease tension and pressure. Prepare a room in your heart to cool down when the heat is up! "A cheerful heart is good medicine" (Proverbs 17:22, NIV).

Step 10: Rise to the Occasion

You can do it! I am excited about what God is going to do in you and through you on this journey. You may take a few detours along the way and even get off on the wrong exit ramp occasionally, but God is right there with you, always ready to guide you back to the right path. He will stretch you beyond your comfort zone and give you the resilience and strength to go through all the bumps along the way. Trust Him on this journey. Seek Him with all your heart. Turn to Him for your stability and security. Embrace the changes this move will bring as an opportunity to learn and grow personally in ways beyond what you could ever imagine.

I will be your cheerleader along the way. I believe in you! I'm standing on the side of the road cheering you on.

And now, with each room you have prepared in your heart, you can move on with confidence. You go, girl!

Moving Right Along

Hopefully, by first taking the time to prepare your heart emotionally and spiritually, you are ready for the chapters ahead as we begin to focus on your child's journey of moving. However, you may still feel you want to learn more about how to personally go through the process of letting go, starting over, and moving ahead with your life after a move. If so, I encourage you to read my book *After the Boxes Are Unpacked: Moving On After Moving In* (Focus on the Family Publishing).

In the next chapter, let's begin to take some steps that will prepare your child for the big moving adventure ahead.

Moving Closer Together

1. Which room will you prepare in your heart?
2. What specific thing will you do to take care of yourself?
3. Share your feelings about this move with someone this week.
4. Acknowledge your fear(s) to God. Then release the fear(s) to Him.
5. Call a friend and share a need.
6. Give yourself permission to cry.
7. What Scripture verse(s) will encourage and comfort your heart?

CHAPTER TWO

Getting Your Ducks
in a Row:
Be Prepared

I started crying when my parents told me we were
going to move and I kept saying no, no, no!
LINDSAY, AGE 16

Our son, Bill, was going into the seventh grade when we told him we were going to move from Atlanta to Phoenix. His response was to turn around and walk out of the room, not saying a word. Our daughter, Ginger, who was going into the fifth grade, seemed bewildered by the whole thing and kept repeating, "Why, Mama?"

Everything Is Not Just Ducky

Each move would always bring a different response from each of us. From tears to excitement, from joy to sadness, I watched Bill and Ginger, at different ages, go through them all. Sometimes just hearing the word *move* would numb me all over. My mind would whirl between the reality and the denial of knowing how huge an impact that one little word would have on our lives as a family.

With my husband, Bill, in the hotel business for most of our married life, moving occurred about every two to three years as part of climbing the corporate ladder. I came to expect it, but dread it. I'd get excited and then I'd get mad. I'd look to the future with hope and then live in the past with regret. Many times I would be the one to say, "Do we have to go?" even before our children would say it!

Once I moved beyond the numb stage, it was obvious that getting my ducks in a row would involve a lot more than just making lists and packing boxes. Regardless of why you are moving, or whether you are moving across town or across the country, don't underestimate the

Six fun things for kids to do to prepare for moving

- Decorate a big box with stickers and crayons for packing special possessions.
- Print or create cards with their new address to give to friends.
- Find out all about the city or town they are moving to. Make a list of fun things to do and places to go.
- Give their friends postcards already stamped and addressed.
- Create a special bulletin board for the whole family where anyone can leave schedules, messages, notes of encouragement, and scriptures.
- Pack a travel bag with their special things to take on the trip when you move. Suggest that they include favorite snacks, books, paper, coloring books, crayons, and other fun stuff.

importance of preparing your children. Moving is as hard for children as it is for adults. Like you, they are leaving behind friends and familiar places. Like you, they have to start over making new friends and adjusting to a new home, community, and even school.

An infant will miss the comfort of familiarity in her old room. A preschooler might worry that toys or pets will be left behind. An elementary-age child could be apprehensive about a different school. A teenager can be moody, withdrawn, and angry over leaving friends and feeling he or she has no control over the situation.

Be Ready for the Storm Ahead

The effect of a move on children can be similar to a natural disaster such as a hurricane, tornado, or flood. No matter how many warnings you get, you never fully realize the magnitude of its impact on your life and those you hold dear. Being properly equipped and prepared to weather the storm, or the move, can leave you and your loved ones bonded even closer by the experience. If you find that the storm, or move, was greater than anticipated, or if you were unprepared, it is more devastating than you could have ever imagined. You are then left with the loss and the brokenness of the disaster.

Be as prepared and equipped as you can for what lies ahead. Don't let this move leave your family in the wake of disaster. The way you handle the preparation time before their lives become disrupted can have a profound effect on children during and after a move.

When Dad told us his new job meant moving, he forgot to say that me and my sister would be going too.

MARK, AGE SIX

What you do and say and how you plan ahead can make a big difference in how your children feel about this move and how they adjust to the transition ahead.

Family Matters

When our family faced a major life change, like moving, we would always gather together and have a family meeting. I'm sure the very mention of a family meeting would conjure up some fear and apprehension about what the subject of the meeting might be, but we believed that being up-front and honest with Bill and Ginger about any issue was important. That way, they would know the circumstances, and we could answer their questions, listen to their concerns, and keep them informed about what was happening. We were careful not to make any promises we could not keep. We didn't want them to have unmet expectations about moving and then blame us for things not going as promised.

One time we made the mistake of promising Ginger all her dolls would be waiting for her when we arrived in Raleigh, North Carolina. Unfortunately, the box of dolls was somehow lost in transition and did not arrive at our new home. (I don't think she forgave us until she was old enough to understand what really happened!)

Hopefully the following tips will help in the beginning stages as you prepare the hearts of your children for the move to come.

Share the news with everyone in the family as soon as possible. There will be at least three questions you will need to answer:

1. Why are we moving?
2. Where are we going?
3. When will we move?

Spend some time explaining each answer and give as much information as you can. The more time your children have to process everything you've told them, the better. So many kids and teens wrote me and said how they wished their parents had told them about the move sooner. They said it would have helped them to have more time to be prepared.

Keep everyone up-to-date by informing them daily or weekly about what is going on. Kids don't like surprises when it comes to life-changing events.

Make this a team effort by involving them in the moving process. Give your children simple, not overwhelming, tasks to be done in their own time frame, such as returning library books or going through old toys, games, and clothes they have outgrown to pass on to someone else. They might want to make up their own checklist and keep it in their room. Involving your children will encourage them to take ownership in the move. If they are part of the process, they will less likely be critical.

Share stories of your own childhood moves. Children love to hear about their parents' adventures in moving. Sharing experiences about how you felt and what you did when you moved as a child will help to bridge mutual understanding and create a common bond. Josh, age eight, wrote, "My dad told me he moved when he was about my age and he didn't like it either. It made me feel better. Then he told me funny stories about his family's long trip from California to Florida."

Give a little extra time. You might need to spend some extra one-on-one time with each of your children. It could be at bedtime, going out for an ice-cream cone together, going for a walk, or sitting around the kitchen table. Buying lunch for our teenagers always worked for us!

Focus on the positive. Talk it up, not down. There's always something positive about wherever you are moving. Think of one good thing each day about moving or find out one interesting fact about where you are

---

Six ideas from parents who've moved

- We showed them maps of our new state and city.
- We took our children along when we went house hunting.
- I included my teenage daughter in some decisions before I moved.
- We told the kids what to expect.
- We tried to keep life as normal as possible.
- I listened and reassured a lot.

going. Share it together as a family at dinnertime. It might do you some good also!

Check out where you are moving. Find out all you can at the library or on the Internet. Books with pictures are great for visualizing a city or state. It's amazing what the Internet will tell you about an area. Write the chamber of commerce and have information sent to your children. (They get mail!) Its job is to make a city or community inviting through brochures and pictures. You can even order a telephone directory for your new city. The yellow pages will really help you get a perspective on the city. Any of these things will help diminish the fear of the unknown.

The Woman in the Mirror

If I could be with you in person right now, I would take out my mirror and ask you to look in it and tell me who you see. Of course it's you! That's a reminder of who the most important influence is in the life of your children. They will mirror what you model. For example, if you are excited and see the move as a wonderful new opportunity, it is likely your children will too. Remember, your attitude and behavior are contagious. If you reflect a negative attitude and act stressed or anxious, they probably will do the same. How you respond will affect their thinking and behavior. Ask yourself, "What am I modeling to my children?"

I never ever thought we would move. This is our home here.
STEVE, AGE 14

Linda and her family moved to Florida recently, and I asked her how she liked living near the ocean. She commented that the weather was hot and humid, the sand was everywhere, and she was so unhappy living there. On another occasion, I was talking with her eight-year-old son and asked how he liked living in Florida. His exact reply was, "The weather is hot and humid and the sand is everywhere. I don't like living here!" He recited his mother's very words. "If mama isn't happy, nobody's happy," as they say!

One More Thing

A very organized mom getting ready to move said to me in a precise manner, "Well, we've got all our ducks in a row. We're ready to tell the kids about the move, make it a team effort, keep them informed, tell all our old stories about moving, have one-on-one time together, check out where we're going, and be positive!"

I responded rather quietly, "But you've forgotten to say one thing, and to do one thing." She leaned toward me in curiosity as I continued. "This is what I would say to my children: 'One thing that will never change is my love for you. No matter where we go, how far away it is, what kind of house we live in, or how many changes we have to make, I will always love you. It's like God's love for us. His love never changes (Malachi 3:6). Nothing can separate His love from us. No matter where we go or how far away we live, what kind of house we live in or how many changes we have to make, God will always love you too'" (Romans 8:35 and Jeremiah 31:3).

Then this is the one thing I would do for my children: I would pray for them. I would take all my preparation ducks and line them up one by one and then give them to the Lord in prayer. The best way to prepare is to pray . . . the first thing every morning and the last thing every night (1 Thessalonians 5:17).

Oh, how I love the opportunity to add that "one more thing"!

In the next chapter, we'll share how to help your children say those good-byes to friends and family before you go. Our journey together as we prepare the hearts of your children for moving has just begun.

Moving Closer Together

1. What is your biggest challenge as you prepare your children for moving?
2. List specific ways you can pray for each other in preparation for the move.
3. Have your children share their biggest fear about moving.
4. Tell them about your moving experiences as a child.
5. Take this opportunity to talk about God's unchanging love for us.
6. Read the Scripture verses in this chapter together as a family.

CHAPTER THREE

Handle with Tender Moving Care: Saying Good-Bye

The hardest thing about my move was saying
good-bye to my friends and family.

THE NUMBER ONE RESPONSE FROM KIDS IN OUR NATIONAL SURVEY ON MOVING

Anne was five when her parents moved from Louisville, Kentucky, to Dayton, Ohio. Her mom, Lou, thought Anne was adjusting well, but she came home one day from kindergarten and burst into tears. Lou asked her what had happened to make her cry like that. Anne's tearful reply was, "When we moved, I lost everything! I lost my house. I lost my friends. I lost my teacher. I lost my school. I lost my street. And now, I've even lost my Southern accent!" As Lou looked back, she realized that to Anne, losing her Southern accent meant she had lost the very essence of who she felt she was. "I wish I had known then what I know now about moving and recovering from the losses you feel when you move," said Lou. "Perhaps I could have given more comfort to my hurting child."

Anne may have been only five years old, but she had great insight about the losses we experience from a move. Regardless of our age, from child to adult, moving can often leave us feeling that we have lost a sense of who we are as a person. To children or teenagers, their home, friends, school, teachers, church, community, activities, and yes, even their accent, are part of the picture of who they are. With the finality of saying good-bye to everything that is a part of their world, that picture is shattered.

Children and teenagers are too young to realize that life is a series of good-byes and new beginnings. They cannot comprehend that life will go on, they will survive, and eventually the picture of who they are will come into focus and take shape again.

For additional insight, let's take a look at some special people and places that are part of the picture of your child's world. Later we'll talk about how you can give your child tender loving care before a move.

Saying Good-bye to People Who Matter

Family, friends, teachers, coaches, and neighbors are just a few of the many people who help connect the dots in your child's world. When your children have to say good-bye to people they love, and those who have had an impact on their lives, it leaves them with a sense of sadness and can make the move itself a traumatic event. For many children, it's the first time they have experienced loss and grieving, and they need an extra measure of tender loving care, packaged with comfort, sensitivity, and understanding. Perhaps you can see your own children in one of these stories:

Maggie, age six, and her parents lived near all her aunts, uncles, and cousins. They were a daily part of her life. When Maggie's parents told her they would be moving, she cried herself to sleep every night. She didn't understand why all her cousins couldn't go with her. "Isn't it like a family vacation and then we'll all come back home together?" Maggie said in her confusion.

"What if nobody speaks to me and nobody likes me?" said Kay, age

10, to her mom. "What if I don't make any friends? I'm so scared to move!" Her world included four close friends that she grew up with in the same small town. This was her family's first move, and Kay's fears were overwhelming.

For Steve, age 17, his basketball coach at school had become a mentor and role model since his parents' divorce. It was devastating for him, living in a single-parent home, when his mom told him they had to move so she could find a better-paying job. Steve was not only grieving the loss of his coach and role model, but a beloved mentor.

The neighbors who had become like grandparents to eight-year-old Casey and his younger sister tried to comfort them with hugs on moving day. Casey and his sister began to cling to them and would not let go of their surrogate grandparents.

There is never enough time to say good-bye.
ERIKA, AGE 17

Our children, Bill and Ginger, were blessed to have the same teacher during elementary school in Georgia. Cindy was not only a wonderful teacher who had a great impact on our children; she also became a family friend and someone we all loved. I remember how we cried when she came to our house to say good-bye when we moved. Afterward, silence filled our home, as if there had been a death in the family. (To this day, we still keep in touch with Cindy.)

Depending on their ages, children will respond differently to the loss of people they have become attached to. Preschool children (ages three through five) don't understand the reality of moving and can't comprehend what the move involves. Reassure your preschooler that moving does not mean separation from parents, siblings, pets, and toys (unless you will be leaving some of those behind). Emphasize that you will be together, only in a different place and a different house. A preschooler's whole world is her family, and she needs to know her world will not be changed by moving.

School-age children (ages six through 12) are focused around the family, but friends and school are also an intricate part of their lives. Our daughter, who was in the fourth grade when we moved to Arizona, left behind her "best friend in the whole world." From walking to and from school to playing together daily, the two of them were inseparable. "My life will never be the same without Kanata," said Ginger. "I'll never find another friend like her!" Saying good-bye to each other brought many tears and much sadness that lingered for months for both girls.

Moving can have a huge effect on teens (ages 13 through 18), and many resist the changes that it brings to their life. At an age when teenagers are beginning to exert their independence from family and develop close relationships with their peers, the picture of their world becomes like a kaleidoscope of emotions. They are saying good-bye to their friends, perhaps even a love relationship, and an identity they are struggling to establish. A teenager's response to moving might be withdrawal, emotional outbursts, acting out, rebellion, or resentment.

You can't help but feel the emotions of Elizabeth, age 15, through her writing:

> I sat on my bed and wept silently, crying out to God. "Why is this happening? Life was so perfect, but now . . ." my voice wavered, and my cry trailed off. A few hours ago, my life had run smoothly. A few hours ago, I had felt secure and on top of my world. A few hours ago, I had not known that I must leave my friends, my school, and my life in Toronto forever. . . . Why must this be? Soon these thoughts spun out of control and filled me with an attitude of anger and resentment.

Tender Loving Care

I have found that it is difficult for children of any age to understand and grasp life beyond who they know and love at this time and place in their lives. Many cannot yet comprehend that with all endings come opportunities for new beginnings.

I encourage you to get in the trenches with your kids. They need sensitivity, comfort, and understanding, along with your tender loving care. Listen with your heart. Let them know that the moving blues are normal. Reassure them that you understand by sharing that you will miss your friends, too. Remember, as difficult as it is, "closure" with friends and extended family is a necessary step to embracing what lies ahead.

Create a safe atmosphere where your children can talk about their feelings without guilt or fear. Let your faith shine. Be an example of a mom who puts her trust and faith in God, the Friend who is always there for us.

Meaningful Ways to Say Good-Bye

First, have your children make a list of everyone they want to say good-bye to. Then, either buy or make an address book (this can be a special project) for names, addresses, phone numbers, birthdays, and other things to remember about each friend. Don't forget that some friends might have e-mail addresses, too. They can send "e-hugs" to stay in touch!

Gather together to celebrate good friends and good times. This could be anything from a pizza party, a sleepover, a "build your own ice-cream sundae" party, or an open house. (It might be easier if you don't call it a farewell party.)

Make the effort to visit and say good-bye to anyone of significance in your child's life, like a teacher, coach, pastor, youth leader, neighbor, or mentor.

Remember your child's friends with a small gift of friendship, or have a picture taken for a remembrance. One of our moving friends made a picture magnet of their children for our refrigerator.

A handmade gift from your child is especially meaningful. Make a bookmark with a special handwritten message and a picture as a keepsake. You can have it laminated at a printing store.

Remembering the Places You Love

The places your children leave behind are an important part of their good-byes as well. Anything that gives the picture of your children's world significance and form becomes a part of who they are. It helps define their lives, just as people do. Some of those places could be your home, a favorite room, the yard, your church, the street where you live, a park, the school, or even a friend's house. (Add your child's own list.) Saying good-bye to any place that is special to your children is an important part of closure.

A creek ran through our backyard when we lived in Georgia. Oh, how Bill and Ginger loved that little creek! I watched them from my kitchen window as they walked across carefully placed rocks to the other side. I could hear them giggle as their feet got wet or as they played by the edge of the water. The sound of rippling water over the rocks muffled out the noises of the neighborhood and seemed to soothe

Care package of tips

- A reminder to you and your children: Grieving for friends and family is normal. It's okay to cry. Your friends and family are worth every tear.
- Comforting with loving arms speaks volumes.
- Laughter can soothe the heart. Laugh a lot.
- Spend one-on-one time with each child. It makes each one feel cared about during the chaos of a move.
- Learn to read behind your children's eyes. It's amazing what you will learn.

all who played there. It soon became Bill and Ginger's special place in the world.

On the day the moving van came, we walked down to the creek together as a family. Each of us shared a special memory of the creek as we threw a pebble in the water. We left behind our "memorial markers," an idea taken from Joshua 4:7 ("These stones shall become a memorial"). Then we walked across the rocks one last time and headed back to our house, with only the noise of the rippling water in the background. Now, after all these years, it takes only a moment for all of us to recall that little creek, the sadness of saying good-bye replaced with the joy of remembering.

Ways to Remember Special Places

Take a picture of your children at a place they want to remember.

Make a video tour of a place to remember.

Keep a memento from that special place. Our son still has an Atlanta Braves souvenir cup from a baseball game.

Take a rock (smooth if possible) from the yard, the neighborhood, the school grounds, or the community as a keepsake of that place. Have your child write the date on one side and a favorite scripture reference on the other side. We have stopped the car alongside the road on the way out of town and picked up a rock to keep!

Children can write in a journal about special people, places, and memories they have in their community. Include in the title the name of the city and the date. The journal becomes a cherished reminder of that place in the years to come.

Cherishing the Memories

We have many cherished memories of every place we've lived. I'm sure our children do, too. Memories are a part of life and of moving. They help connect the dots of the past. "We're making memories" is a phrase that has been passed down in our family for three generations now. I remember my mother saying those words to my brother and me. I say it to our children, and I've overheard them saying it to their children!

The hardest thing about moving is leaving everything you know and love. At least that is what happened to me.

PAIGE, AGE NINE

When Bill and Ginger were younger, they would roll their eyes when I brought out the camera for a memorable moment, or suggested we were making a memory around an event in our lives. But now, those pictures or events, places, or things have become a part of our cherished memories and link our hearts and emotions to the past. It is also part of a rich heritage that makes them who they are. So "let's make memories" for your children to take with them! Here are a few "memory makers":

Have friends sign an "autograph shirt." Every time your children wear it, they are getting a "friendship hug."

Pass around an autograph book for friends to sign. Ask for a picture to go along with the autograph.

Put together a scrapbook of memories. Be sure to date the pictures and events.

Create a special memory box filled with meaningful things.

Leave behind something that symbolizes your family's presence there. Sometimes we've planted a bush or a flower in the yard. Ginger has left notes in her room for the new occupant. We've even buried a jar with a note in it in the backyard!

At an outside farewell gathering, give everyone a helium balloon with a long ribbon attached. Each person shares a send-off wish or prayer for the person moving, then releases the ribbon and the balloon is sent off as a symbol of blessings for the future.

At this very moment, my friend, you might also need some tender loving care as you struggle with your own good-byes. Even though I am talking about your children, I have not forgotten you. As I am writing, I always have you on my mind. I understand the tightrope you walk in balancing your own emotions and feelings, while at the same time trying to encourage your children. Do not lose hope; God will fill the emptiness in your heart and the loss of friends and family in your life. He will replace your good-byes with hellos in due time. In the meantime, let Him care for you as only He can. An old hymn, "Leaning on the Everlasting Arms," says it best for me. The words always come to mind when I need to be reminded that His arms are waiting to care for me . . . and for you, too.

What a blessedness, What a peace is mine,
Leaning on the everlasting arms.
What have I to dread, what have I to fear,
Leaning on the everlasting arms?
I have blessed peace with my Lord so near,
Learning on the everlasting arms.

In the next chapter we'll talk about what to do to pave the way for a smooth move. The road ahead can be bumpy, but we'll be ready!

Moving Closer Together

1. Name some of the people that you and your children will miss the most. Talk about why.
2. Discuss how you are going to tell friends and family good-bye.
3. Take time out to visit a special place your children love. Linger a while and savor the moment.
4. Decide how you will make memories to take with you when you move.

5. In Genesis 12:1, who moved away from his family and friends and a place he loved? Who did he take with him? How do you think they felt about moving?
6. Who not only said good-bye to His family, friends, and home on earth, but gave His life for you and me? (John 3:16) Why?

CHAPTER FOUR

A Smooth Move Can Have a Bumpy Start: Paving the Way

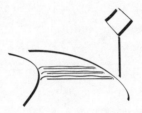

I remember what a really hard time my mom
went through when we moved.
COLE, AGE 15

Before we move along any further, let's take a deep breath together and take time out from all of our to-do lists. Let's just take a minute or two and visit. We're coming up on Part II soon, and I want to help you pave the rest of the way with a solid foundation. Even though this book is about helping your children through the moving process, I keep coming back to you for a reason. You are the one who is encouraging your children hands-on, face-to-face, and one-on-one. I want to continue encouraging you as a moving mom, heart-to-heart and page to page! Remember what I said before. I care about you!

Bumps Along the Way

It is my desire to equip you to have the smoothest move possible for your family. However, I know there are things in life that can give even a smooth move a bumpy start and a bumpy ending. Sometimes your move is not about a job promotion, but a job loss. Sometimes it's not about two parents moving with children; it's about one parent's struggle to hold the family together. Sometimes moving is about difficult circumstances, like illness, death, or divorce.

It could be an emotional issue, like the pain of separation from family, fear of the unknown, or anger and resentment about moving again so soon. To add to that, there could also be struggles in your marriage or with a rebellious teenager. To some moms, the bumps are more like mountains. Along with all the moves that are wonderful and exciting, anticipated and planned for—even dreamed about—there are also the moves that are heartbreaking.

You keep me in the reality of both "moving" worlds. I've read your letters and e-mails as you've poured out your hearts, I've heard your broken voices on the phone, and I've seen your pain face-to-face. Eight out of every 10 of you who contact us at N.E.W. Ministries have had a difficult time in your transition and adjustment to moving.

I know you are out there. You've somehow found this book and then this chapter. For all of you who feel that this chapter is not about you or your move, you may be surprised. Even the good moves are about change, and with change comes an adjustment in some level of your life. So change is what I want us to talk about for a while. Read on, my friend.

The Things You Cannot Change

What's going on in your life right now as you prepare for this move? Do you have any issues, circumstances, or feelings heavy on your heart that you would like to change but can't? I kept these words taped on my refrigerator for many years until the paper began to turn yellow from age: "Lord, help me to accept the things I cannot change. Give me the courage to change the things I can, and the wisdom to know the difference."[1] I've had to learn those words the hard way through many moves, and many times at the expense of my family. It took years for me to finally get it.

I couldn't change the circumstances when Bill lost his job and we had to move again within 18 months. I couldn't change my heartache when we moved 3,000 miles away from my mother, who was very ill. I couldn't change the feelings of anger, resentment, and loneliness after so many corporate moves. I couldn't change the distance between Bill and me each time we moved, even though we lived under the same roof. I let my pain, my emotions, my anger, and my resentment seep into my relationship with Bill and our children. I couldn't change my circumstances to make life and moving easier, no matter how hard I tried.

> *I kept trying to make my children happy when we moved. I finally realized that was impossible. Some of it was up to them.*
>
> KAREN, A MOVING MOM

Through the years, I did learn about "the wisdom to know the difference" phrase in that prayer. Perhaps wisdom has a lot to do with getting older, or perhaps it's a function of time, but I believe the difference in knowing and accepting what you can't change is wisdom of the heart. First, God changed my heart, and with a heart change, there was a gradual change in me. I began to look at my circumstances with His perspective and through His eyes rather than mine.

I went to Him when I didn't have all the answers and couldn't change what was going on around me. He became a Friend in my aloneness and my Comforter through His Word: "If . . . you seek the LORD your God, you will find him if you look for him with all your heart and all your soul" (Deuteronomy 4:29, NIV). I then slowly began to live above the things that I could not change, not below them. I began to realize that I could not change the bumps in the road as we moved, but I could change me.

You can have a bumpy start, even a bumpy ending, but you can pave the way to a smoother move by asking God to change your heart and to give you the wisdom to know what you can and cannot change along the way. As the popular saying goes, "Give it up." Give it all to Him. He can carry your burdens so much better than you can. He can give you the strength to face whatever lies ahead, and He will accompany you on the journey: "I will . . . make the rough places smooth" (Isaiah 42:16, NIV).

Spell It Out!

Take the following acronym for the word *change* to heart and pass it on to your children. You might want to write it on a 3 x 5 card as a family reminder. When going through change in a move, remember this:

C ling to God! Hold on to Him with all your strength. He is your anchor in the storms of life. Just as a vine clings to a tree and becomes entwined as one, so should you with God.

H e is immovable! You are the one moving; God never moves from you. You can count on Him to be there at all times. His presence will never leave you.

A lways trust Him! God is trustworthy. You can trust Him with everything in your life and with this move. Trust that He knows what lies ahead and trust that He will take care of your family. He will not let you down.

N ever give up! When the road gets rough, don't give up. Stay strong and persevere. Press on, keep moving forward, and keep your eyes focused on the goal ahead.

G od will make the "rough places smooth"! He promises! Be reassured as you read His Word and abide in Him.

E xpect a few bumps on the road! The reality of life is that everything will not go smoothly all the time. If you expect some bumps along the way, you can be prepared, have a plan, and pray, pray, pray!

Pave the Way with Positives

My dear friend Nancy said to me recently, "Your mother taught you early in life how to embrace change. Her positive attitude helped you over the years in the adjustment of moving. When I was a child, my mother just 'folded' each time we moved, and I grew up thinking moving was the worst thing in the world." Nancy's words were a good reminder of the impact we have on our children and how what we say and do can affect their thinking as adults.

It's important to remind yourself and your children of the positive aspects of moving, even in the middle of the bumps along the way. The changes that come with moving can be good for you and your family, and the benefits are endless. For many families, it is an opportunity to start over with a clean slate. It can be a great way to broaden your world by meeting new people, making new friends, and being exposed to a new culture and lifestyle. The choices and circumstances that surround your kids in moving teach them life lessons that are invaluable. They will become more sensitive to other kids who are in transition, and they will become better equipped to cope with change.

Moving can definitely take you out of your comfort zone and stretch you beyond what you think you can do. What might emerge is a new and stronger person. It can be an opportunity for personal growth and learning through all kinds of opportunities. It can even strengthen and unite the relationships within your family. Leslie Levine says it so well in her book *Will This Place Ever Feel Like Home?*

Moving is a great leveler. Barriers are broken. Clarity is achieved. We even get to know ourselves a little better. As we examine the many changes that spill forth, we hone our ability to cope. While sorting through these changes, have patience and be mindful of the ripple effect. Trust your intuition and have courage that you will persevere.[2]

When you are a newcomer, schedules, commitments, and calendars haven't started robbing your family of time together. When all you have is each other to rely on, it's amazing how you will bond together. I remember our traumatic move from Georgia to Arizona. It was one of those "How can I ever be happy again?" moves for me. In His time, God provided friends who have become like family, brought Bill and me closer together, and broadened my world from just Southern culture to Southwest culture. Never underestimate what God can do!

Here are several things you and your children can do to pave the way to a smoother move:

Pray out loud for one another for specific moving concerns.

Schedule family time to work through any moving issues.

Take turns sharing favorite scriptures of encouragement.

Affirm your commitment to one another during this transition.

Make it a habit to have a family devotional time together.

Give lots of hugs.

Remember the meaning of the acronym CHANGE every day!

Someone passed these words on to me years ago. I thought it would be a perfect ending for chapter four. My prayer is that it will help you understand the things you can do and the things you cannot do for your children. May these words written by an unknown author minister to your heart as you "pave the way" to a smoother move.

The Limits of Parenthood

I gave you life, but I cannot live it for you.

I can teach you things, but I cannot make you learn.

I can give you directions, but I cannot be there to lead you.

I can allow you freedom, but I cannot account for it.

I can take you to church, but I cannot make you believe.

I can teach you right and wrong, but I cannot decide for you.

I can buy a beautiful garment, but I cannot make you beautiful inside.

I can offer you advice, but I cannot accept it for you.

I can give you love, but I cannot force it upon you.

I can teach you to share, but I cannot make you unselfish.

I can teach you respect, but I cannot force you to show honor.

I can advise you about friends, but I cannot choose them for you.

I can advise you about sex, but I cannot keep you pure.

I can tell you the facts of life, but I cannot build your reputation.

I can tell you about drink, but I cannot say NO for you.

I can warn you about drugs, but I cannot prevent you from using them.

I can tell you about lofty goals, but I cannot achieve them for you.

I can teach you about kindness, but I cannot force you to be gracious.

I can warn you about sin, but I cannot make you moral.

I can love you as a child, but I cannot place you in God's family.

I can pray for you, but I cannot make you walk with God.

I can teach you about Jesus, but I cannot make Jesus your Lord.

I can tell you how to live, but I cannot give you eternal life.

What's the first thing you do when you're not sure how to get to your destination? You ask for directions! As we move on to the next chapter together, you'll not only get the directions for your family's journey; we'll map it out one step at a time!

Moving Closer Together

1. Ask each family member what bumps he or she is worried about. (A bump is anything that would keep a move from going smoothly.)
2. What will each of you do to pave the way ahead?
3. Tell how you think this move will bring about positive change in your children's lives and in your life. List three specific things

that will be positive. List three things that you are looking forward to.

4. Read the first part of Malachi 3:6 out loud: "For I, the LORD, do not change." What reassurance in the midst of change does this scripture give you?

5. Memorize Proverbs 3:5-6 (NIV): "Trust in the LORD with all your heart and lean not on your own understanding; in all your ways acknowledge him, and he will make your paths straight." Remember, He will pave the way, as you trust in Him!

6. Write down Acts 17:28 and put it where your family will see it every day: "In him we live and move" (NIV).

PART II

During the Move . . .

"Are We There Yet?"

CHAPTER FIVE

Ask for Directions: The Best Way to Get There

Where do we go from here?

MARTY, AGE NINE

How many times have you started a trip in the car to an unfamiliar place only to realize you are either lost or not sure of the best way to get there? I can only laugh at the number of times my husband, Bill, would not stop to ask for directions, but try to figure it out himself. It must be a "guy thing." I, on the other hand, would roll down the window and ask strangers on the street corner how to get somewhere. It makes a big difference who is behind the wheel in our car!

More Than One Set of Directions

My mother frequently asked, "How do you get there from here?" when she needed directions. That question, "How do you get there from here?" can take you down many roads and a lot farther than just miles. What directions or guidelines do your children need to get from "here to there" spiritually and emotionally? In other words, what do you want them to learn during this moving experience that will strengthen their faith and help them become better, not bitter, movers?

I'll never forget what a moving mom told me years ago. "If only I had known then what I know now," Linda said as she reflected back over her 10 moves. "Our four children grew up during our corporate moving years, and I missed the opportunity to teach them some valuable things that come from a moving experience."

I don't want you to miss the opportunity. Let's assume you are behind the wheel at the moment and you are ready to ask for directions for the journey ahead. These directions on "how to get there from here" will impact your children's lives long after you've arrived and settled in. It's not always the destination, but the journey, that is often most remembered.

We're in This Together

When our children were younger, we would take them camping and white-water rafting in North Carolina. Our one goal, one focus, and one purpose was to get down the rapids with everyone still in the raft and without the raft tipping over. I vividly recall my fear that one or both of the children would fall out or that Bill and I would not be able to hold the raft steady and we would all go overboard. Of course our biggest obstacle was outside the raft, the raging rapids around us. Our raft ride was an incredibly bonding experience. We were all paddling in the same direction, and we all had our part in the plan to get us to our destination.

The same principles can apply to the moving experience. (You might even want to use the analogy of the raft story for a visual effect.)

The plan is to arrive at your destination healthy, all in one piece, and still speaking to one another!

Just as in the raft, each family member has his or her part to play in the move, while pulling together as a team.

All of you are in this move together, regardless of the external (and even some internal) circumstances trying to pull you apart.

As parents, you are committed to each of your children from start to finish, through the smooth times and the rough times of this transition.

Moving is one of life's experiences that can either bring the family members closer together or drive them apart in the process. You have an important role in the direction your children will go. Your commitment at the beginning—to see them through until the end, no matter what it takes or how long it takes—will move your family closer together through this experience.

> *Mom, isn't there a shorter way to get there?"*
> LISA, AGE SEVEN

This Too Shall Pass

Sometimes it's hard for children to grasp that there will ever be an end to sad feelings about leaving behind all the people and things they love. Teenagers might think that their lives have fallen apart and that they couldn't possibly ever be happy again.

It helps to put the move in perspective. I like to draw a big square on a piece of paper and tell children (and moms) that the square represents the big picture of their life. Then I draw a small square in a bottom corner as I explain how that small square represents their move. The move is only a small part of the big picture of their life. Assure your children that God is big enough to cover all the corners and spaces and places in their lives with His love and comfort during this transition. The crisis of moving will pass, but God's love is here to stay.

Remember What's Important

What's important to you? I like to ask that question of women who are moving, to hear their responses. Some of them say a favorite piece of furniture or a picture on the wall. Others say it's their grandmother's china or a favorite keepsake. It's always interesting that when you're packing up and moving belongings, you become overly attached to the things that seem to identify who you are. It's as if your identity is being stripped away in a move and suddenly the things around you become magnified in importance. I've felt the same way too. "Oh, my mother's antique punch bowl or that dining room set that I waited forever to get" was my typical response.

The interesting thing is, what becomes important to us becomes important to our children also. We are our children's greatest teacher, and they learn by example and modeling, even during the transitions in our lives. Let's rethink what is really important. What would you tell your kids really matters when things are stripped away in a move?

Your faith and God's faithfulness

Your Bible, God's Word

Your prayers and God's promises

Your family and God's blessings

Your values and God's principles

Your morals and God's commandments

Your love for each other and God's love for you

Long after my dining room set and antiques are gone, these are the things that will still really matter and that I take with me wherever I go. How about you?

Look Ahead, Not Back

Your children will have a difficult time getting "there" from "here" if they are always looking back over their shoulder. I know it's easier to look back where life was clearly defined, especially when the visibility on the road ahead is not real clear. It's easy for them to compare the old with the new and the best with the worst. This only makes starting over harder and moving on with life more difficult.

A visual picture I like to use with kids (and moms) is taken from Psalm 61:2: "Lead me to the rock that is higher than I." Picture God taking your hand and then leading you to a giant rock, one that is even bigger than you are. You climb up on the top of that rock, stand up, and to your amazement you can see the view ahead. It is so much better and so much clearer than before. You just needed to see the view from another position and another perspective.

Pave the road ahead as your family's big adventure. (We'll talk more about this in the next chapter.) Remember, you're all in this together. Enthusiasm is contagious!

There Are No Shortcuts

It's only natural to want to get to the other side of an unpleasant situation or difficult circumstances as quickly as you can. We all want to avoid the tough issues or the painful feelings that accompany a hard journey. But unless you are going to live in the "state of denial," the only way to get to your destination is to go through the experience. What a valuable life lesson for your children to begin to understand through this move. When you encourage them to face the emotions and feelings about moving and deal with the issues and the situations in moving, you will then begin to build openness, trust, and coping skills within the family unit. That sense of "we're in this together" and a family oneness emerge.

God will use this experience in your lives to teach each of you things He could teach you no other way. In one of our moves when money was tight, God taught us day by day about His provision. Each one of us learned how God truly does meet all of our needs, but not necessarily all of our wants!

Walk with your kids through this transition. Don't try to shortcut the experience.

We're Gonna Make It, One More Time

Maybe this is your second or sixth or even 10th move. Maybe you feel like you don't have the strength to do this one more time—but you do, and you will. As a moving mom, I believe in you. You've got what it takes. You will persevere and get through it. Your determination to make it will allow you to rise to the occasion. Now go tell your kids that you believe in them and that they've got what it takes to make it through this move. And make sure you tell them, We are going to make it—one more time!

A wise person once told me that God doesn't give us a map of our lives that we can see from beginning to end all at once. It would probably scare us! Rather, He reveals our lives one day at a time, much like a scroll that is slowly unrolled. By being able to see only one day at a time, we become more dependent on God to help us day by day, and less dependent on ourselves. We have to trust Him for each day and for tomorrow. George MacDonald said it well: "Care for the next minute is just as foolish as care for tomorrow, or for a day in the next thousand years. In neither can we do anything; in both God is doing everything."[1]

As the old saying goes, "We do not know what tomorrow holds, but we know Who holds tomorrow!" So, my friend, put your trust in God to lead you, guide you, and give you direction in the days ahead. He will reveal to you the best way to get there from here!

A Map for the Journey

These scriptures will help map out your journey ahead regardless of your destination city. If you begin to lose your direction, don't worry; God has your forwarding address!

"I will instruct you and teach you in the way which you should
go; I will counsel you with My eye upon you" (Psalm 32:8).

"Let your eyes look directly ahead and let your gaze be fixed straight in front of you. Watch the path of your feet and all your ways will be established" (Proverbs 4:25-26).

"The mind of man plans his way, but the LORD directs his steps" (Proverbs 16:9).

"Your ears will hear a word behind you, 'This is the way, walk in it,' whenever you turn to the right or to the left" (Isaiah 30:21).

"I am the way, and the truth, and the life" (John 14:6).

"You will make known to me the path" (Psalm 16:11).

"Thy word is a lamp unto my feet, and a light unto my path" (Psalm 119:105, KJV).

"LORD, thou hast been our dwelling place in all generations" (Psalm 90:1, KJV).

"The LORD will guard your going out and your coming in from this time forth and forever" (Psalm 121:8).

"Where can I go from Your Spirit? Or where can I flee from Your presence? . . . If I dwell in the remotest part of the sea, even there Your hand will lead me" (Psalm 139:7, 9-10).

"The steps of a man are established by the LORD, . . . the LORD is the One who holds his hand" (Psalm 37:23-24).

I know how you feel right now, as though your whole life is in brown boxes and you don't belong anywhere—not where you came from and not where you're going. Remember, this too shall pass. You won't hear "How much farther is it?" (in chapter six) much longer. And you and your family will arrive (in chapter seven), whether you're traveling by land, air, or sea.

What will your children do until you pull up in the driveway of your new home? Lots of practical ideas for the trip are coming up in the next chapter.

Moving Closer Together

1. What's the "best way to get there from here" for your family?
2. Discuss three key things you want to learn as a family from this move.
3. Talk about how you can best pull together as a team.
4. What are some circumstances or situations that could pull you apart?
5. Verbalize your commitment to your children before, during, and after this move.
6. Draw the big picture of life with the move as one small part, then talk about it.
7. Have each person tell what's important to him or her in the process of moving.
8. Now talk about what really matters.
9. Tell your children you believe in them.
10. Write the list of scriptures in "A Map for the Journey" on 3 x 5 cards and read one at a time to your family during your move.
11. Pray for direction and guidance in the days ahead.

CHAPTER SIX

How Much Farther Is It?
On the Road or In the Air

I rode in the backseat of our SUV with our two cats, two ducks,
and a dog when we moved from Kansas to Arizona.
LAUREN, AGE 17

We named our small used Toyota "the brown berry." We always named our cars. We kept our cars so long that to us they were like part of the family. When Bill Jr. and Ginger were very young, they thought it was funny for our cars to have names. When they got older, they simply became amused at one of their mother's crazy family traditions. (I bet that they secretly name their own cars now.)

During one move, Bill started to work in North Carolina before we actually moved there. Once everything was packed and the moving van was on its way, I set out to drive the brown berry across three states loaded down with two kids, a dog, and boxes overflowing in all directions. Bill Jr. was six and Ginger was three. I don't remember how old the dog was.

What I do remember was our road trip. It was extremely hot and the

53

brown berry came down with heat exhaustion. (That's what I told the kids.) In adult language, the air conditioner quit blowing cold air. Oh, it would still blow air; it was just hot air. So I rolled the windows down to let the hot air out only to find the air coming in was even hotter.

At that point, Ginger, who was sitting in the backseat, started throwing up all over herself, her doll, and the seat. Bill Jr., who was sitting in the front seat, started gagging at the smell, and the dog had his head hanging out the window drooling from the heat. I don't think the smell bothered him. We were not at a place where I could pull over, so with Ginger now crying, Bill Jr. gagging, and the dog drooling, I was held captive at the wheel.

While I was thinking *What else could possibly happen?* I began to imagine Bill sitting in a new air-conditioned office somewhere. I started getting furious at him for not being there to share in this memorable experience. At that same moment, the brown berry must have gotten a tummy ache (that's what I told the kids) because the red light came on indicating that the engine was overheating. We kept limping along in all our glory for miles until we came to an exit with a gas station. There we found a quick fix for the brown berry, a clean restroom with lots of paper towels, and a grassy spot for the dog. As we got back in the car, Bill Jr. said for the hundredth time, "Mom, how much farther is it?"

I'm sure you can identify with my road trip in some way. We all have our moments of traveling chaos and calamity that eventually become memories to share and laugh about. In this chapter we'll prepare for the trip ahead and offer some practical ways to ease the miles to your new destination.

Car Conversation

Don't miss this window of opportunity. It's amazing what you can learn about your kids by simply listening while you're on the road or in the air. Kids are most likely to feel safe and comfortable in the environment of a car or sitting next to you on the airplane where they have your undivided attention. Settings like this help to promote an atmosphere of openness and vulnerable sharing. Even listening to conversations between siblings becomes a source of greater insight into their world and their thinking.

Carol, a moving friend, tells about the time her two daughters were talking in the back of the car as the family made their way across Texas to California. The girls somehow started talking about things they were

Mom, I think one of our suitcases just fell off the top of the van.
Bill, age six

afraid of, and then shifted the conversation to their fear about moving. They began to pour their hearts out to Carol as never before. For the first time she had real insight into what they were thinking. "I really believe being in a close setting in the car, with my one-on-one attention, released any self-consciousness to share their innermost feelings," she said. So instead of dreading cross-country trips, make the most of talk time.

Tips for Travel Talk

Be a focused listener. Go easy on asking a lot of questions.

Turn off your cell phone. Make calls when you stop for a break. This is the time to focus on your kids.

Tune in their music. Take this opportunity to discuss the songs and lyrics.

Designate a time frame for personal electronics. Take a time-out from electronic games and CD players.

Point out things of interest along the way. They can be great conversation starters.

Ask questions that require more than a "yes" or "no" answer; for example, "Tell me about . . ."

Make It an Adventure!

Start paving the way by saying, "This is our *big* adventure!" long before your trip begins. Building enthusiasm produces excitement for what is to come. Even if you have to look for the positives, learn to "make lemonade out of lemons."

Everywhere you go and everything you do along the way can become your children's big adventure, including going to the airport to catch a plane and dealing with the luggage and long lines. Whether you are stopping along the roadside or at a park for a picnic, going sightseeing in a city, or just taking a break at a restaurant en route to your new residence, make it an adventure for your family.

Make It Fun!

Long hours on the road or in the air can be very tiring for children. They can easily get cranky or irritable, which can have a ripple effect on the whole family. The more you have planned to help pass the time, the easier the trip will be. It could be as simple as what Sarah's mom, Trina, did for her when they moved to Singapore. "I remember my mom giving me little trinkets here and there to help me through the 20-hour plane ride. About every two hours my mom would surprise me with a little gift that would entertain me." Sarah was 10 at the time, and now at 17, she still remembers how that idea helped her through the long flight.

Here are some other ideas from moms on the move that you might want to consider:
- "We took along books on tape for our two teenagers." Barbara, New Jersey
- "Don't forget the basic card games, puzzles, and board games that don't have a million pieces." Jen, Alabama

- "When we have a long trip cross-country, our kids always take their own tote bag with electronic games, radios, CD players, CDs, and headsets." Chris, Arkansas
- "We gave our teenager a map of our trip and asked him to pick out some sightseeing places along the way. It made him feel like he was part of the decision making for the trip." Kelly, Nevada
- "We almost forgot our children's pillows to take in the car." Jean, Ohio
- "We made $8^1/_2$ x 11 copies of a small map of the United States. Each day our kids wrote a note to friends they left behind and showed them where we were on the map. We would postmark the letter from that city." Wanda, Georgia
- "Our kids took backpacks on the airplane filled with their own snacks, books, pens, paper, coloring books, small handheld games, and cards. That way they could do their own thing from their own backpack." Laurie, Colorado
- "We gave each child a sketch book of their own with washable markers and crayons. We suggested they draw and color pictures of their new home, their room, and the yard along with pictures of our family moving in." Janet, North Carolina
- "Make the move a vacation by planning to stop along the way, if time permits, and see some of the places your children have learned about in their history or geography classes. Even if you haven't planned ahead, stop if you see signs for interesting historical markers, sights, towns, and overlooks." Kathy, Colorado

Make It Meaningful!

One of my favorite things to do during a move, or anytime for that matter, is to go on a "God hunt." This is something parents and children can do that will give each person the opportunity to look for God in everything. It also helps your children think about seeing God in every aspect of their lives. Some of the ways to go on a "God hunt":

"I see God in the beauty of the sunset."

"I see God in our move. He did . . ."

"I see God in this day. Look what He did . . ."

"I see God in every detail of this move. For example . . ."

"I see God taking care of us on this trip. He has . . ."

"I see God in you!"

Car Games to Entertain Ages Three and Up

As the road seems to get longer, the kids might need to stretch a bit, wiggle their fingers and toes, stretch their necks from side to side, and play a few games. Try these for fun:

Someone picks a color, like red. Then everyone looks out the window for anything that is red. Keep score of how many objects are found by each person in a certain amount of time.

Look for cars that are all a certain color, have license plates from the same state, are the same kind, or have luggage racks on top. You can add your own list of similarities.

Look out the window and try to find shapes of animals or other objects in the clouds.

Kids take turns "packing the moving truck" by adding an item each time they get a turn. Then the next person has to repeat all the items packed before adding one more to the list. When a player misses an item, he or she is out of the game. ("I'm packing the moving truck, and I'm going to pack my toys." Next person says, "I'm going to pack my toys and games.")

It's also fun to pack the moving truck in alphabetical order.

Look for cars with license plates from different states. Each state is worth 10 points. The first person to see a state plate gets the points.

Once that state is used, it cannot be used again. At the end of the trip, the person with the most points is the winner.

Another fun thing to do with license plates: Write down some license plate letters. Then think up words and phrases using all the letters. The first person to complete words and phrases for all the listed plates is the winner.

Have fun with bumper stickers. Look for different bumper stickers and write down what they say. Two people cannot claim the same sticker. The person with the most stickers wins. The players can also look for stickers that contain things in common, like a heart, a color, or a number. (Be mindful that some bumper stickers are not suitable for children.)

Travel Tips from Experienced Movers

Moms are always sharing their travel tips with me to pass on to other movers. You might want to remember these great ideas as you plan for packing the car:

A kitchen timer can be used on a trip in several ways: "It's your time to share" or "We'll stop for a break when the timer goes off."

Take a roll of paper towels, small garbage bags, wet wipes, and Ziploc bags in the car for cleanup, diapers, and trash. You'll be glad you did!

Air freshener really comes in handy. It covers food odors, plus all those other unpleasant smells we don't have to mention.

A first aid kit. Make sure the one you have is not outdated.

A cooler with favorite snacks, juice, fruit, and sandwiches. Include a heavy-duty Ziploc bag filled with ice to soothe any minor bumps, cuts, or scrapes.

For long trips, take several gallons of water. Small bottles of water don't last very long.

Don't forget a small water bowl for your pet. Put someone in charge of keeping your dog's leash. When he is desperate to get out of the car, it helps to know right where the leash is located.

When you are staying at a hotel overnight, stop late in the afternoon in time for the kids to go swimming and work off some energy before bedtime. Get up for an early departure to get a good start on the day. The kids might sleep through the first few hours of the morning.

Seize the Day!

Whether you are traveling in a car or an airplane, encourage your children to take the time to practice acts of kindness, be thoughtful of each other, and show a little extra patience. When everyone has been traveling for hours or days, a little kindness, thoughtfulness, and patience go a long way. Don't miss a moment of opportunity that could make a difference in the entire day!

Judy's family had been on the road for their third day as they made the trip from Washington to New Mexico. Everyone was worn-out and irritable. The twins, Mike and Jeff, were arguing in the back of the van when their older brother, Tom, turned around and intervened by offering to play a game with them. At the same time, one of the twins accidentally hit Tom on the head with his elbow. "That's okay," Tom said. "I know you didn't mean to hit me. Now let's find a game to play." Judy was relieved and happy to hear how Tom resolved the argument and responded to being hit in the head. "It was amazing how pleasant the rest of the day was!" Judy said.

Are we there yet?
GINGER, AGE THREE

Seize the moment or the day to make the best of a situation and model to your children how they can show kindness, thoughtfulness, and patience on a long trip.

In the next chapter, we'll take a look at how to get your children settled in after you arrive.

Moving Closer Together

1. Share your biggest concerns about the trip. Talk about how you can avoid those problems.
2. Practice these words: "This is our big adventure!"
3. Start your trip with a "God hunt."
4. Choose a game or two ahead of time that everyone in the family can participate in together.
5. When everybody is in the car or airplane, give an example of what it looks like to be kind, thoughtful, and patient with one another.
6. Before you begin the trip to your new destination, pray together as a family.

CHAPTER SEVEN

What Do I Do Now?
We've Arrived!

We're here now. I like it. We're living in an apartment
with a swimming pool. Thank You, God, for making
everything go so smoothly.

LEXI, AGE SEVEN

We pulled up in the driveway of our new house. The trip had been long and hot, but we had made it safely, and for that I was most grateful. In their excitement, the children jumped out of the car and ran to the front door, long before Bill could get there with the key. I slowly got out of the car and took a quick look at the front yard and the house that would soon become our new home.

The yard definitely needed a little work. The front porch needed some flower pots. The shutters could use a new coat of paint. My mind began to form a checklist of things the eye could see. At the top of my list was the heading, Where do I begin? This is where I started.

Celebrate!

As I said before, "If mama isn't happy, nobody's happy." Oh, the truth in those words. As a mom, you set the atmosphere in your home during the moving process.

I know we've talked about this before, but you must never underestimate the importance of your role as a mom in the life of your children. Your attitude, your actions, and your words are contagious. Regardless of why you moved, this is a new beginning for all of you. Make the most of it by celebrating your arrival. Here are some celebration ideas:

Buy some helium balloons and tie them on the mailbox.

Make a poster that says, "Welcome to the Neighborhood" and hang it on the front door.

Open a bottle of sparkling cider and let everyone "toast" the family's arrival, new home, and new beginnings.

Order pizza and stick one candle in the middle to represent your first night together in your home. Or you can buy a ready-made cake and put candles on it to celebrate.

As you walk from room to room in your house, pray God's blessings over the future use of each room. Specifically pray for the activities, family, and friends that will become a part of your home. This is a meaningful time for everyone in the family.

Order in Your Child's World

Before you tackle unpacking the boxes, consider what Margi, who recently moved to Michigan, does after a move. "We try to concentrate on the kids' rooms first since they need to settle in as soon as possible. I help them open their own boxes and place their clothes in the drawers so they know where to find things when they need them. Once they know all their things have arrived safely and they know where to find everything, they feel better. This will free me up to take care of the rest of the house with fewer interruptions."

Another mom, Sherry, who moved to Tennessee, says, "We encourage our kids to unpack their tote bags or backpacks first, and put all their treasures out in the room to give them comfort. It helps to have their familiar things around them."

Sometimes you can let your kids choose their own bedrooms and help arrange the furniture. It's wise to hang pictures and put the toys away. Some teenagers might like to set up their room and choose the paint or wallpaper. The teens that are electronically minded can be given the task of setting up any electronic equipment, like computers, stereos, TVs, VCRs, and DVD players. Older kids might like to make some baby-sitting money by watching the younger ones while you are unpacking.

The first night your children spend in their rooms, surprise them with a little note in a card, or a special treat left by the side of the bed or on the dresser. It could be as simple as a single flower (in any kind of container that's unpacked) or some cookies on a plate. Use your creativity. It is knowing you did something special just for them that will help ease the transition of the first night in new surroundings.

Other ways to ease the transition are by being available and by being willing to listen, which is not always easy when you are going in a hundred directions with a list a mile long. However, the list will be there tomorrow and is filled only with tasks. Taking the time to be available allows your children to look in your eyes and see a piece of home. Listening gives you a window into their thoughts.

In the busyness of getting settled, don't overlook these two things: your presence and the assurance of your love. I always told our children that they were never alone—that I carried them in my heart and was with them in spirit. One way I reassured them of my presence when we were apart was to say, "I'm a little bird, sitting on your shoulder. Look too close and you'll knock me over." It is kind of corny, but I repeat it often to friends and family for the need of the moment!

Bringing order to your children's world when you arrive will provide them with a solid foundation in adjusting to their new environment.

Order in Your Home

I know—all the boxes did not go away overnight! Wouldn't it be a dream come true if everything was suddenly unpacked and put away in the right place? Wishful thinking will not make it happen. It takes time and hard work.

In the book *Smart Moves*, coauthor Audrey McCollum writes, "A couple who share the work, the pain, and the joy of moving set a fine example of teamwork for their children, and are better able to support their children through their transition."[1] It takes a joint effort at some level of participation from everyone in the family to transform a house into a home.

When the children observe both you and your husband working together toward a common goal, they begin to grasp the concept of "we're in this move together." Involving your children says to them that their feelings and opinions are important to you, and that they are part of the team.

If you are a single mom, get some help as you begin to move into your home. You cannot physically do all that needs to be done by yourself. Involve your children, according to their ages, to help with some of the tasks. Don't think you have to do everything alone. Remember, you and your children are a family. Make your move a team effort. In addition, ask around for resources or support. Consider these suggestions:

- Call the youth department of a local church. Teens are always looking for ways to make a little extra money. If you can't afford to pay for help, let the youth director know. Many teens will volunteer as part of serving in the community.

- Ask your neighbors or people you work with for assistance or referrals.
- Check out "moving services" in the yellow pages for help unloading.
- Look for "handyman" services in the yellow pages. They'll not only help unload, but can also hang pictures and check out your home maintenance if needed.

Unpacking Fun

Unpacking can be fun for your children rather than something everyone dreads. Margi came up with a fun idea to entertain her two children. She sent them on a "moving label hunt." She gave each of her kids a blank piece of paper with their name on it. They each took the paper around the house looking for all those little numbered labels the moving companies put on furniture to inventory the items.

The kids would peel the label off the object and place the label on the paper. When they finished unpacking, she counted up the labels and gave them a dime for each label. It gave them a fun way to help.

Annette, from Texas, let her kids play house or build forts with a few of the empty boxes before she threw them away.

What's Next?

After you have unpacked and stuffed the wrapping paper back in the boxes (don't you feel like you are knee-deep in all that paper?), put bandages on your fingers from the paper cuts. Then you can try to figure out where to put everything that fit in a room in your old house but doesn't seem to fit in the new one. Oh happy day!

As you begin to bring order out of chaos, look around. Does every room hold something—a picture, a keepsake, a remembrance—that your family loves, something that warms your heart or makes each of you count your blessings? When life has been disrupted in a move, being near things that you and your children love brings comfort and helps to restore your family. Your home is a sanctuary from the world, and how it makes you feel emotionally and physically is far more important than how it looks. Stephen Covey says in his book *The 7 Habits of Highly Effective Families,* "Creating a warm, caring, supportive, encouraging environment is probably the most important thing you can do for your family."[2]

~

Being with someone you love is being home.

TOMMY, AGE SEVEN

~

More Than Unpacking Boxes

Bringing order to your home is not all about unpacking boxes. The kind of order I am referring to is the consistency of love, care, nurture, protection, and stability that the world does not offer. It is a home where calm lives over chaos and where hope lives over despair. It is a home where the teaching of Jesus Christ is modeled and lived out daily through your parenting. Living out the teaching of Christ takes you beyond providing the physical comforts of a home. Your life becomes a reflection of Him as you:

show love to one another;

choose joy instead of complaining;

let God's peace, instead of fear or worry, fill your heart;

practice patience as you wait for everything to come together;

reflect kindness and gentleness through your actions;

demonstrate faithfulness by believing and trusting in God, even though you can't see results;

express self-control instead of outbursts of anger when things don't go according to your plan;

exemplify high morals, honesty, and integrity in every area of your life.

Standing in the Middle of a Mess

I remember when I was newly married and pregnant. I was totally confused by all the books and magazines I read on how to be the model wife, be a super mom, have a perfect home, and make big bucks. It was then that my beloved daddy took me aside and said to me, "Everything you want to know about marriage, parenting, home, children, and finances can be found in the Bible. All you have to do is read it with your eyes, believe it with your mind, and apply it with your heart."

You may be at a time in your life right now where you feel the same way I did so many years ago. You're confused by all you read and hear. Everybody is telling you something different. You don't know what or who to believe. You feel like you are standing in the middle of a mess that is far more significant than boxes to be unpacked.

The answers you are looking for are so easily attained. God is just waiting to tell you how to be a loving wife and mom, how to get those boxes unpacked without losing it, how to have order in your home . . . all this and more, just for the asking. You see, the more you ask of God, the more He gives. He shares His wisdom with you in the same Bible from which He shared His wisdom with me. Read it, believe it, apply it!

Routine Is Important

The quicker you can get back to familiar routines, the more comforting it will be for your children. It will give them a sense of connection from the routines in their old home to the routines in their new home. In the midst of change, routines within the family are reassuring that life is getting somewhat back to normal. The routine of dinnertime, when everyone eats together, brings continuity to the end of the day. The routine of your children setting the table or cleaning up the kitchen reestablishes responsibility.

I always took Bill and Ginger's artwork and pictures off the refrigerator whenever we moved and put them in a plastic bag for safekeeping. Putting everything back on the new refrigerator let them know that some things never change. Try to recreate the pattern of your child's life as much as possible.

Traditions Live On No Matter Where You Live

Sarah, the daughter of my friend Trina, recalls when they moved to Singapore. The first thing they did was to go on a search for great hot chocolate, something Sarah loved back in the States. "And sure enough, God provided. Our favorite coffee shop in San Francisco had just opened a store about five minutes from our house in Singapore. It was our sign that God wanted us there."

Finding good hot chocolate was a tradition that brought the familiarities of home back to Sarah. That's what traditions are all about; they are our connection to the past and a warm remembrance of a familiar ritual in our lives. Just as moving interrupts our lives, traditions within the family can connect us again.

Each time we moved, the first thing we did was to hang up our hammock between two trees. The hammock has been a tradition in our family for generations. My grandmother had a hammock that I would swing in as a child. My mom and dad continued the tradition and passed it on down to us. When our children got married, we gave each couple a hammock. The tradition lives on, with cherished memories woven within each fiber of our hammock.

Home is what catches you when you fall.
KATHY, AGE 10

Even though traditions are a part of the past, it's never too late to start a new one within your family now. Sue started the tradition of making chili for her family's first night in their new home. They have moved 12 times as a military family, and chili has become their traditional first meal, no matter what season of the year!

Kara and her young daughters have started the tradition of planting bulbs as a reminder that they will all be growing in their new environment. A "Moving On" scrapbook filled with pictures and stories from their four moves is a tradition Michelle started for her children. The Willis family takes a cement stepping-stone with the imprint of their child's hand to every place they move. What a perfect time for your family to begin a new tradition or a ritual with this move. It will enrich your children's lives—and your own.

In the next chapter we'll talk about how to plug your kids into the community and get them started off on the right foot. So let's all "hold hands and stick together" as we move into Part III.

Moving Closer Together

1. Reflect on this scripture: "I will walk within my house in the integrity of my heart" (Psalm 101:2). What does this mean?
2. What were some of the emotions each family member felt when you arrived at your new home? (This is a good discussion topic for the dinner table.)
3. How can you best support your child at this time?
4. How will you reflect Christ to your children? Discuss how they can reflect Christ to one another.
5. What is a tradition or ritual you have in your family? Discuss with your children new ideas for a tradition. Get everyone involved.
6. Read Psalm 37:3-5. Meditate on each verse. What does it tell you to do now that you have moved?

PART III

After the Move . . .
Hold Hands
and Stick Together

CHAPTER EIGHT

Starting Off on the Right Foot: Plugging In

We just moved to Texas. I joined Brownies, and it is fun.
We have not found a church yet, but we are still looking.

SIERRA, AGE SEVEN

We've gotten past the front door now; past the few boxes that are left unopened. It looks as though everything is beginning to come together. But is it? It doesn't matter if the curtains are up, the pictures are hung, the flowers are planted, and the wreath is on the door; if you find that your family is disconnected since you moved, what else really matters?

Yes, you do need to learn your way around the city, find an aerobics class, check out the shopping malls, and call that new neighbor for lunch. However, let's "plug in" with family first. After you move and bring some kind of order to your home, take a look around and see how the people who live there are really doing. After all, that's the best way to start off on the right foot.

Be There for Your Children

My friend and mentor over the years Dr. John Trent has written many books that have had a profound effect on our life as a family. One in particular caught my eye as I walked by our bookshelf. The title alone captures the essence of what I want to convey in this chapter. In his book *Be There!* Dr. Trent shares how you can make a difference in the lives of your children and your spouse by "being there" to connect with them emotionally and spiritually:

> It all begins with a choice. Being there for your child means: choosing to connect with him or her, being alert in the present moment, and meeting a need or making a positive contribution, regardless of the cost.[1]

After moving, the connection to family is vital to the physical, emotional, and spiritual welfare of your children. At a time when the family unit can become fragmented and is often fragile, to be there for each other can both settle and stabilize a child's world. "The move brought my family together in a new way," said Elizabeth, age 15, "and our relationships with each other improved. My father's new career change meant less travel and more time with the family. Having him at home now caused me to realize the extent to which I had been numbed to his absence. It became clear to me that without our relocation, my relationship with my dad would not have been renewed, and I would have missed out on so much joy."

It takes time, effort, planning, and even sacrifice for you and your spouse, or for you as a single mom, to be there for your children. There were those times that I wasn't always there for our children after we moved. I was either struggling emotionally, too focused on getting our house decorated, or trying to fill up an empty calendar out of loneliness.

Oh, I was there to fix meals, take them to school, run errands, get them to activities, and make the orthodontist appointments, but I missed the connection in being there with them and for them one-on-one and eye-to-eye. I didn't take the time to look beyond their eyes and see into their hearts.

Here are some of the ways Dr. Trent suggests in his book that you can "be there" for your children:

> Compliment each of them individually every day.
> Compliment and encourage your spouse in front of the kids every day also.
> Give them a hug or other special touch each day.
> Point out to them that they have a special future and purpose.
> Set aside time each week to work on a project with the kids.
> Plan alone time with each child.
> Read books, play board games, take hikes, ride bikes, or blow soap bubbles.
> Take your kids to church and volunteer in their Sunday school classes.
> Read one Bible story or chapter together a couple of times per week.
> Pray with and for your children each morning or night.
> Take time to share with them what God is teaching you during your week.[2]

God's Design for Marriage

It has been said that the greatest thing you can do for your children is love your spouse. I believe those words with all my heart. I know without a doubt that it has been my love for Bill and his love for me over the years that has created a sense of security for our whole family. Our love for each other holds our family life in place even in the midst of change, crisis, and turmoil. Of course we have had our share of problems and conflicts, but underneath it all was the safety net of our committed love for each other. Ginger said to me recently, "Mom, when Bill and I were growing up, everything in our life was always either up or down—grades, school stuff, friendships, sports. The constant in our life was the security, stability, comfort, and encouragement you and Dad provided. That's what I want my marriage to be like and what I want to give my children."

I know in my heart it was God who covered our many flaws and imperfections as parents. All the times we didn't do it right, or couldn't get it together, He would cover us with His grace and love. Only through Christ could we emerge whole in our brokenness as parents, and in our marriage. Here are some ways that you can strengthen your marriage after a move:

Start daily devotions and couple prayer times. (I read somewhere that couples who have daily devotions and prayer time together have a divorce rate of one in a thousand.)

Pray for and give thanks for each other.

Improve communication by having weekly catch-up conversations.

Keep short accounts with each other: "Do not let the sun go down on your anger" (Ephesians 4:26) or any other unresolved issues.

Schedule time for a date night.

Learn each other's love languages. (See Gary Chapman's *The Five Love Languages: How to Express Heartfelt Commitment to Your Mate.*)

Plan a getaway for just the two of you.

Look for the "stress cracks" in your mate. (Is the job working out? Is everything coming together at home?)

Be there for each other and let your kids see that you are.

Mr. Rogers' Neighborhood

When you step outside your front door and look up and down the street, wouldn't it be wonderful if Mr. Rogers were to appear to welcome your children to the neighborhood? For most of us, Mr. Rogers' perfect neighborhood lives only in our hearts and memories. The neighbors who do come to greet you and your family when you move in are indeed a treasure in this day and time. When they bring a gift that says "Welcome" or offer a kind gesture to assist you, it is something you never forget.

We live in neighborhoods of isolation—with walls and fences around our yards, and garages that we open, drive into, and then shut without even getting out of the car. Our backyards, rather than front yards, have become our family gathering places. With so many two-income families, there is hardly anyone left on the street during the day to notice a moving van coming or going. But do not lose heart! Neighbors are there, and like you, would probably love to meet and greet others. But you just might have to be the initiator. These suggestions could help you meet other moms with kids and help connect kids to kids:

Be proactive. Don't wait to be asked; have a "come on over" attitude. Create an invitation on the computer or make a flyer to distribute around the neighborhood inviting moms and kids to a get-acquainted party. Be creative.

Open up the garage, carport, or driveway area for a monthly (or weekly), totally casual Saturday morning coffee-and-donuts drop-in. Moms, dads, kids—everyone is invited. Soon, word of mouth will make your yard the place to be for a visit!

Be bold for your kids. Step out of your yard and step up to a neighbor's door. A playmate could be a knock away.

Look for clues in the neighborhood that indicate children live there—bikes, toys, playground equipment, and baby strollers. Don't forget the biggest clue, a large vehicle like a van.

Walk your younger kids to the school-bus stop in the neighborhood.

Take a walk down the street and around the corner on a Saturday. People are more likely to be out in their yards then. Always speak and introduce yourself as the new neighbor; don't miss the personal contact opportunity.

Borrow an egg—or anything that will give you the chance to meet a neighbor.

Set up a lemonade stand in your yard or driveway. Kids have a way of attracting other kids while doing fun things.

Ask the mail carrier who has kids on the street.

Look for a playground area nearby.

Three important things you can do: Find a church, find a church, find a church! If it's summertime, inquire about vacation Bible school for kids. Ask about church camps for junior high and high school. This is a great way for your kids to meet other Christian kids in the area.

Check out the Moms in Touch International Web site at www.momsintouch.org for a moms' prayer group that meets in your area.

Check to see if Young Life, a Christian organization for junior high and high school kids, is offered in your area. For more information, go to www.younglife.org.

Put On Your Tourist Hat

It's time to explore! Remember the "big adventure" we've talked about? Well, now is a good time to take your kids on a big adventure to discover what's out there in your new state, city, or town. This is all a part of the process in connecting to their new world. As your family becomes familiar with the surroundings, they will begin to feel more comfortable in their new environment, and then new roots will begin to grow.

Don't leave home without it—a map, that is. Make sure you have a city map, a state map, or a community map, depending on which one you might need. Keep all maps in the glove compartment of your car. They won't do any good if they're left at home. (Guess how I know that!) Use bright-colored markers to map out the way and stickers to mark the destination.

Plan ahead and gather as much information as you can. (You should still have the brochures that you sent for from the chamber of commerce before you moved.) Check out the yellow pages to get an overview of what's available locally: restaurants, toy stores, video-rental places, library, community and recreation centers, parks, and other special places that might interest your children. (Make the library a priority, and get your family library card.)

Going online is also a great way to find out about your city or state. The local newspaper will tell you what's happening in and around town. Keep a small pad of paper in the car or in your purse for specific directions or phone numbers, then take the small-step approach by going to some of the places. You don't have to see everything or go everywhere in one day. That could be overwhelming to a young child. (And yet to a teenager, it could be stimulating.) It's always good for the kids to have something to look forward to next time you plan a big adventure.

> *It is in the shelter of each other that the people live.*
> IRISH PROVERB

Make sure you stop for lunch or a treat and share about a favorite place you've been that day. It might be fun for your kids to take some pictures to send back to their friends, telling them all about the new place.

In time, the world around you will become familiar. The attachment to places you frequent will grow, and you will begin to feel a sense of community and home. In the meantime, enjoy being a tourist.

Now that we have "plugged in" to our family, neighborhood, and community, let's talk in the next chapter about a huge issue in the life of your children—making friends.

10 Secrets of a Happy Family That Moves Closer Together

1. Instill a strong spiritual foundation.
2. Enter into each other's world of interests.
3. Look for ways to have fun.

4. Laugh a lot together.

5. Tap into the power of touch; hug or hold hands.

6. Take the time to affirm, praise, encourage, and value one another.

7. Focus on what's good about your kids.

8. Say "please" and "thank you."

9. Demonstrate an observable love.

10. Hold hands and stick together.

CHAPTER NINE

The New Kid on the Block:
Making Friends

Mommy, making friends is easy; you just smile,
tell them your name, and be nice.

ADVICE FROM TY, AGE SIX

"What was the hardest thing about moving?" I asked.

"Leaving friends," they answered.

Then I asked, "What is the hardest thing about moving to a new place?"

And they answered, "Making friends."

These are the identical words that I read and heard hundreds of times in surveys and in interviews from kids of all ages who had moved.

You understand. You've been there emotionally, or perhaps you are there right now. You find yourself still struggling with your own sadness over leaving old friends. At the same time, you're wondering if there is someone out there who one day you will be able to call "friend."

You desperately want to help—want to do something—anything that might help your child get through this difficult time of building new relationships.

Where Do You Begin?

In your eagerness to help your children, remember the things you cannot do, as well as the things you can do, in the process. You cannot speed up time, and it takes time for everyone to settle in, adjust, and make friends. As coauthor Thomas Olkowski says in his book *Moving with Children*, "You cannot fashion your children's adjustment or manufacture their happiness with your new surroundings anymore than you can go out and create new friendships for them."[1]

What you can do, though, is to offer your reassurance and some simple suggestions in how to begin the friend-making process. You can pray faithfully and be there to listen and encourage. You can refresh basic social skills, such as how to start conversations, as well as build up your child's self-confidence through affirmation and praise.

Each child's friend-making ability is unique by age and personality. Since preschool children don't know how to introduce themselves, you need to get them together, teach them each other's names, and play games with them. This helps them become comfortable with each other.

If your children are between the ages of six and 12, try to get them involved in after-school groups such as a youth group at church, Scouts, or organized sports. Most of the time, elementary-age children lack the social skills to make a stranger feel welcome, so the new child is often left out. Don't completely rely on the playground at recess or school activities to be the source of friendships. Invite someone your child has met to come over for a visit. Often that one-on-one time will be the beginning of a new friendship.

Need I say that teenagers are a whole different story? Carolyn Janik shares in her book *Positive Moves* that teens find moving more painful than any other age group. They are at an age when they are forming an identity apart from the family and with their friends. Jeanne, who is a sophomore in high school, said, "I felt stable and happy with my friends and myself. I wasn't ready for that to be taken away from me by a move." Moving means that ties to a teen peer group will be broken, and your teenager is once again dependent on the family as the only support system. Sparks can fly along with the ebb and flow of emotions. If you have a teenager, you understand what I mean. Teens can become rebellious and resentful and the whole family can feel the effects of their outbursts. What they don't realize, Janik says, is that "teenage friendships rarely survive a move by more than six months. In six months new friends may be more important in their life than the friends that are left behind. Some things in life one must discover for oneself."[2]

When we moved, we encouraged our son to participate in both a team sport (or another group activity) and an individual sport (or activity) in high school. That gave him the opportunity to meet and interact with a number of other teenagers as well as one-on-one. It also taught him how to be a team player as well as build confidence in an individual sport.

We made an intentional effort for our house to become "the hangout" for Bill and Ginger's friends when we moved. Food and a listening ear were always available at the Millers' house, along with unconditional love and a nonjudgmental spirit. Somehow they kept coming back for more. Many a teenager slept on our sofa and floor during high school. Things haven't changed that much over the years; teenagers still want a safe place to be, unconditional love, acceptance, a listening ear—and food. Try it. It can work in your home, too.

Things Kids Want You to Know

As a mom, sometimes you don't have a clue about what to do or say, or what *not* to do or say to help your child in the friend-making process. These are some things kids who have moved wanted you to know:

Give me time and space. I need to adjust to my new surroundings first.

You don't have to have all the solutions for me as I try to make new friends. Sometimes I need to do it on my own.

Please don't pressure me into activities I'm not interested in or am uncomfortable doing, just to make friends.

The way I approach making friends is different from my brother because I'm not like he is—I'm shy.

You are my only friend right now. Will you take a minute from your busy schedule and talk to me?

Don't assume there is a problem just because I like to spend time alone. As long as I am happy, it's okay.

I need some downtime without scheduled activities, and especially some quiet time with you.

Let me go back and visit my old friends if it's possible.

Back off a little bit. I'll be fine now. The worst is over.

Lighten up, Mom! You are worrying too much.

"Kids' Tips" Straight from Their Lips!

I'm passing on these tidbits for your kids, from kids who have moved. It will help them know what to do and what not to do as they begin to make new friends.

What to do:
- Talk to people. Introduce yourself and ask their names. Then as an icebreaker, ask questions about them such as, "How long have you lived here?" Or ask directions to a place. Say something that makes them feel good about themselves like, "I really like your outfit," or "You are a great soccer player." To start a conversation, you have to talk!
- Smile. A smile breaks down barriers and invites a "Hello."
- Be friendly. To make a friend, you have to be a friend.

- Be nice, pleasant, and courteous. A grumpy attitude and bad manners won't get you far.
- Remember the names of those you meet. Everybody loves to be remembered by name.
- Be yourself. You can't be everything to everybody, nor can you be someone else. Just relax and be who you are.
- Look for other new kids. There is someone else around who is new just like you!
- Give it time. God has a special friend chosen just for you.
- Try to get involved. Be interested in what other kids are doing. Ask if you can join in their activities. And remember that wearing your Hawaiian shirt in Minnesota might not fit in.
- Don't give up. Try, try, and keep on trying again until it works—maybe with someone else.
- Invite someone along. Ask someone you've met to do something or to go somewhere with you, like coming over to your house or going to an activity.
- Join in and join up. What activities do you like—sports, computers, drama, band, Scouts? Participate with other people.
- Volunteer. Raise your hand high! You might even enjoy helping out.
- Stretch out of your comfort zone. You are the new kid. What have you got to lose? Be flexible. Try something new and different, something that you've always wanted to do. What a time to grow and expand your horizons!
- And for all the kids who might be shy . . . believe in yourself. You have nothing to be afraid of. Making friends is not as hard as it may seem. If you want to make a friend, you'll have to show it. Stretch yourself and make the first move. Take it slow at first and work on being a friend. Get up the courage to introduce yourself and let others know who you are. Show kids you are interested in them and let them know things about you. Don't worry about

being shy. You can always practice talking with your family. That's a great place to start building your confidence. And remember, all of your old friends were once strangers.

What not to do:
- Do not be afraid. Go for it! Get out there and introduce yourself.
- Do not try to impress by showing off. You can be cool, but don't overdo it.
- Do not try to be somebody you're not. Just be you! You are God's original. Don't become someone's copy.
- Do not compare the place you came from with this new place, or the friends, or the school. Nobody likes to feel second best.
- Do not act unusually goofy or silly or make a scene for attention. Weird behavior can be a real turnoff.
- Do not act bossy. Nobody likes to be bossed around by a new kid.
- Do not interrupt other kids when they are talking or butt in when they are doing something. You'll make a bigger impression if you wait your turn.
- Do not hang out with kids that have different morals and values than you do just to be popular. Compromising how you were raised does not justify the need of the moment. You'll end up regretting it and being miserable.
- Do not get into a situation with kids that will affect your lifestyle and lower your standards. The quick fix to being accepted is not acceptable!
- Do not hang out with troublemakers or bullies. They will only make trouble for you and make your life more difficult.

The Best Kind of Friends

What does the right kind of friend for your child "look" like? Your kids may not have any trouble making friends, but your concern is the kind

of friends they will choose. Sometimes children and teenagers who are the "new kids" are prone to get into the wrong crowd just to be accepted and belong to a clique. Friends are as important as parents in shaping your child's sense of self. A friend can validate your child's worth and strengthen his self-esteem, or a friend can tear down his worth and destroy his self-esteem.

The hardest thing about moving was that we couldn't bring our friends with us.
ANNESSA, AGE NINE

Never underestimate the influence of your children's friends. Watch for red flags such as behavior changes, loss of interest in school, and becoming secretive about their social life. If friends seem overly influential and pushy, talk to your child about what a true friend should be:

A true friend is someone who can be trusted.

A true friend will be there in time of need.

A true friend won't encourage your child to do something dangerous.

A true friend won't put your child in a compromising position and won't entice him to make wrong choices.

With true friends, there is mutual respect for each other and each other's possessions.

With a true friend, there is freedom to be the real you.

Although it may be hard to do, try not to judge potential friends by their hairstyle or dress. Sometimes the kid that fits your standard of dress may be the worst person for your son or daughter to be with.

Try to make it less convenient for inappropriate friends to be influential. Find reasons for your child to decline going out with the friend. Set limits and phone curfews. When they do get together, have them do it at your house if possible. The best way to discourage negative peer pressure is through a loving, accepting home and open communication. Neil Bernstein, author of *How to Keep Your Teenager Out of Trouble*, says, "The choice of friends is a barometer for a kid's sense of self. If you don't talk to them, they will talk to anyone who listens, relying on friends for validation, instead of you."[3]

The Roots of Friendship

Just like a tree has to have deep roots to survive the winds of time and seasons of life, your children need to have deep roots when the winds of change and the seasons of transition come. I am reminded of Psalm 1:3: "He will be like a tree firmly planted by streams of water, which yields its fruit in its season and its leaf does not wither; and in whatever he does, he prospers."

You get twice as many friends when you move.

ADAM, AGE EIGHT

When a child's roots are firmly planted in a relationship with Jesus Christ, she begins to understand and grasp our model for friendship. The life of Christ is the template for all relationships. If your children ask any questions about being a friend, making a friend, or having a friend, tell them about the Friend we have in Jesus. Share with them all about His life in the Gospels. Tell them the stories about how Jesus modeled friendship with His disciples; how He shared His life with them, spent time with them, and prayed with them; how He was committed to them, built trust with them, accepted them, and encouraged them.

It is in the context of the family and home that your child develops the roots of friendship. It begins with Jesus and flows through you.

Train up a child in the way he should go, even when he is old he will not depart from it (Proverbs 22:6).

You shall love the LORD your God with all your heart and with all your soul and with all your might. These words, which I am commanding you today, shall be on your heart. You shall teach them diligently to your sons and shall talk of them when you sit in your house and when you walk by the way and when you lie down and when you rise up (Deuteronomy 6:5-7).

Next to friends, the other big issue with kids and moving is school. Naturally, the first step is to identify the best school options for your children. Appendix 3 (page 143) gives lots of practical tips for doing just that and for helping your kids feel comfortable before that important first day of school. But right now, we're going back to revisit school through the eyes of kids who move. I can hardly wait to get to the next chapter with you.

Moving Closer Together

1. Discuss the "Do" list and focus on the ones your child might need encouragement in doing.
2. Discuss the "Do Not" list and talk about the things your child might be doing that he or she shouldn't.
3. Talk about the different ways your child can be a friend and ways he or she can reach out to make a friend.
4. What are the qualities that you look for in true friends?
5. Talk about the kind of friends that you don't want, and why.
6. How is Jesus your Friend? What are some things that Jesus does for you that no other friend can do?

CHAPTER TEN

School Daze:
What If Nobody Sits
Next to Me at Lunch?

Walking into a cafeteria of 1,000 kids and not knowing
anyone—when the other 999 kids do—is beyond intimidating.
JEANNE, AGE 15

"I'll be okay, Mama," Ginger said with an unconvincing voice. My heart was pounding. It was Ginger's first day in her new school. She was going to be in the fifth grade. The ride around the circular driveway to the front entrance of the school seemed miles long. All the faces of the children rushing toward their classrooms were unfamiliar, and I felt Ginger's apprehension about opening the car door and stepping out into the unknown.

I tried to be cheerful, hiding my own fears for her. I knew how important that first day would be to set the tone for the year ahead. I asked if she wanted me to walk with her to class, and she nodded her head that she did. As we walked to her room, I could sense how alone she felt even with the hall full of other kids. Everyone around us was on a mission to get to the right class or catch up to a friend before the bell rang, so I could understand why no one spoke or even acknowledged Ginger's presence. It was as if she were invisible.

When we got to the classroom, I peeked inside the door and caught the teacher's eye, just as she started toward us with a welcoming smile. My mother's heart felt deep relief. I knew she understood. Just before Ginger walked through the door, I bent down to kiss her and whispered, "You'll do great today! I love you, and I'll see you this afternoon!" As I turned and walked away with a knot in my throat, I prayed, "Lord, I'm leaving her in Your hands. Watch over her—and please, let it be a good first day!"

That morning is so vivid in my mind. The first day at a new school was always a milestone for our children in their transition. I'm sure you've shared some of those same thoughts and feelings when you took your children to school, or if you walked them to the bus stop, or said good-bye at the front door of your home. No matter what age your children are, when they are the new kids, the first day of school can be a frightening experience. Be sure to send them off with lots of love, words of encouragement, and an embracing hug that assures them you understand and will be there at the end of the day.

Here's the Scoop

According to the U.S. Census Bureau, more than 13 million people under the age of 19 move each year.[1] As you can imagine, one of the most difficult aspects of moving for millions of children is the adjustment to a new school. The reality is, when you're new at school, academics are not a priority until you have adjusted and feel comfortable in your surroundings. Reading what some kids wrote about their feelings on the first day of school can put things in perspective rather quickly. "I begged my mom not to make me go on the first day of school," said

Lauren, age 16. "I felt rejected, out of place, alone, and lost," said John, age 12. "I walked around by myself, not knowing where to go," said Matt, age 17.

For as many kids who will adjust to school quickly, there are also those who find it very difficult. With some kids, everything will come together smoothly—making friends, feeling accepted, fitting in, liking teachers, and being on track with their classes. For other kids, it's a nightmare. They don't seem to fit academically or socially. Self-esteem and confidence have hit bottom. They long for a good friend. There is no connection with the teachers.

As a parent, you are on a seesaw of emotions along with your children—up and relieved when one of them adjusts well, but down and worried when one of them doesn't. You've probably asked yourself, "Will a balance of emotions and adjustment ever come?" Do not lose hope, my friends. You and I will hold hands and stick together on this one! I'll share with you what I know from my own experiences and what I've learned through interviews and surveys with kids, teachers, and counselors. Help is on the way.

Easing the Transition

Keep in mind that age, personality, and family support are all factors in your child's adjustment to school. Also, just the fact that your child is new puts him or her on the "outside of the circle" of school and friends. Until someone or something opens the circle and includes or invites your child inside, he or she will remain an outsider. In the meantime, what you do to ease the transition into school will give comfort and confidence to your child.

Your children will appreciate your sensitivity in these areas:

Wait until you see the local fashion trends before you go shopping for back-to-school clothes. Fitting in is very important to kids.

Write down the bus number, your address, and a phone number

where you can be reached during the day, and any other pertinent information that your children might not remember if they become anxious or panic. Put it in their backpack or school notebook. When kids are new, it's hard to remember a lot of new numbers.

You might want to consider printing some address cards with each child's name, address, phone number, and e-mail address. They are fun to pass around to new friends.

Ask the teacher to assign a buddy for the first week so your child won't be alone at lunch or at recess.

Lighten up on the academics for a few weeks. It may be more important at first to make friends and learn about the school. Your children will learn a lot more when they feel comfortable and stable in their surroundings.

Words to the Wise Mom

If you're not completely on information overload by now, tuck these few suggestions in your pocket and reach for them when needed:

Don't overlook the obvious. Accompany the kids on field trips, bring goodies to class to celebrate special occasions, or work in a booth at the school carnival. For younger children, find out when you can join them for lunch. Any hands-on involvement is a source of connectedness for you and your child after moving.

Being new can be lonely. (We'll talk more about that in the next chapter.) After school, make sure your children don't come home to an empty house or apartment. If you work outside the home, make arrangements for someone to be there with your child or arrange a planned activity through the school or community for after-school hours. (Community or recreational centers are a good place to start.)

Hopefully you've found a church home by now and your child is involved in a church youth group. This is an excellent way to connect with other kids who are Christ-centered.

Encourage participation in school activities. There is a spirit of camaraderie in being a part of the bigger picture of school life.

Talk about the big picture. You might want to get a copy of last year's yearbook for the teenager in your family. What a great way to "be in the know" at a glance. Find out the "who, what, and where" of the school.

Find the teacher in a gifted program that works with the special gifts your child has and get them together.

For teens, technical support for school productions is a great way to plug in since there are many skills needed to manage the lights, sound, and sets.

Suggest that your son or daughter volunteer to be a buddy to the next new child who comes to school.

I wish the people at my new school would understand more about what I went through as the new kid there.

KELLY, AGE 10

For the younger kids, pack a shoe box with things that are important to them and that will tell about where they came from. Your child can share with the class the first day of school.

Ask your kids to draw and color pictures of their new school and the people in the school. Talk about the pictures; you'll be amazed at what children reveal about themselves through their drawings.

Ask the teacher for a roster of kids in the class for two reasons: (1) The kids can write letters back and forth with a new friend. (2) You can quickly find out which kids live near you to have them over after school.

Remember to pray together and share scriptures of encouragement with your kids.

Straight Talk from Teachers and Counselors

I don't know about you, but as a parent, I've always listened to a teacher's perspective. I could learn something myself. After all, they are with our kids all day and they look at our world as families from a different view—the classroom.

"Every day the number one objective for kids is to get through the day without being humiliated." Terri, high school counselor

"Questions like, Am I smart enough? Will I measure up? Will the kids like me? Will the teachers like me? Do I look okay? can consume the thoughts of new kids." Martha, high school counselor

"Kids need to hear encouraging words at home, like, 'You can do it!' 'You are an asset to the school!' 'Kids need more kids like you!' 'You are a great friend and people will benefit by knowing you!' 'You will get through this!' 'There are other kids going through the same thing!'" Virginia, second-grade teacher

"New kids need to have a sense of hope and anticipation that things will soon be back to normal." Sharon, 10th-grade teacher

"New kids need supportive parents, but not too doting. ('Are you okay?' 'Are you sure?')" Alishia, fifth-grade teacher

"They need lots of pats on the back and a positive place to be themselves." Doreen, fourth-grade teacher

"It would be helpful if parents would role-play various situations at home that new kids might face at school." Lisa, third-grade teacher

"Don't make promises to new kids that you can't keep." Sharman, sixth-grade teacher

"Feeling like they don't fit in is huge to new kids." Jeri, eighth-grade teacher

"New kids need extra love, attention, security, and acceptance." Sue, first-grade teacher

Kids' Comments

Are you ready to hear from the kids? They are ready to talk to you! Like teachers, they can also give us a perspective that we can learn from—the view from their world. You're in for a surprise.

"I'll never forget the teacher who came up to me the first day of school and said, 'How are you doing?'" Jennifer, age 17

"My mom encouraged me every day and told me the next day would be better—and soon it was." John, age 12

"School was really weird the first day." Riley, age nine

"My teacher had a 'new kid' stool that I got to sit on and tell about my move." Adam, age eight (twin of Brian)

"I was really scared on my first day of school—all day." Brian, age eight

"When you go to a new school, go to social events. Don't be afraid to go up to people and introduce yourself. You will find you have more courage than you think." Katherine, age 14

"As a new kid, I played soccer and that really helped." Brett, age eight

"God showed me that I needed to get my security, confidence, and encouragement from Him, and not from a school." Elizabeth, age 15

"Not everyone wanted to play with me at recess because I was new." Alix, age 10

"On my first day of school I was really nervous, but things got better after lunch." Emma, age nine

"I made lots of friends on the bus." Tim, age 11

"I just started a conversation with someone at school and we kept on talking and became friends." Kyle, age 10

"I prayed a lot those first few months." Michael, age 13

"My mom always had a smile on her face when I came home from school, even though I knew she was still sad about moving." Charlotte, age 16

"My world was turned upside down when we moved and I had to leave my old school and friends. My family and my belief in God helped me turn my world right side up again." Crystal, age 14

"My first year in a new school was ravaged with heartache, and yet flavored with joy. It was a year of change and a year of tremendous growth. It was a year in which I learned the immeasurable value in projecting oneself and what one stands for. I learned to celebrate my differences and cherish the differences of others." Christen, age 17

The Four Rs

As you can see from the comments from kids, school is no longer the three Rs, but the four Rs of Reading, 'Riting, 'Rithmetic, and Relationships. Our schools teach far more to our children than just what they learn from textbooks. The world of your children has become much larger than just the family unit. It has expanded to the school, where they face choices daily that can change the course of their lives. It's a place where they can "try their wings" and develop interactive skills necessary for relationships with others. It is where they find a battlefield of experiences—the hard knocks of ridicule, rejection, and even prejudice.

I finally had to let go, trust God, and just be myself in school.
COLE, AGE 15

In the center of their world, the family becomes a place of safety, refuge, and stability. It is the family that provides peace, nurture, and support, while teaching and modeling the truth of God's Word. With all the external influences your children face daily, it will come down to God and family who will remain internally steadfast in their ever-changing world. You are your children's greatest teacher!

A Word to Homeschooling Moms

While the adjustments homeschoolers have to make may be fewer because kids don't have to adapt to a new school, homeschool families must still adjust to a new home and community. My friend Misty, who homeschools her two children, had this to say to homeschooling moms on the move:

The benefit of homeschooling is that once you "set up shop" you can start right back into your schooling routine. Most families need at least a couple of weeks to get unpacked and acclimated before attempting to begin schooling after a move. Give yourself enough time, and don't pressure yourself to get started immediately. Time is a great advantage that homeschoolers have and reduces the stress that can accompany moving. The secure feeling of the family around your children is still intact and dependable. There might be the fear of making new friends, but getting involved in a homeschool group as well as a church will help alleviate that.

If you haven't already done so, research the homeschool co-ops and support groups near you and contact them for information. Depending on your family's need for socialization, academic, or extracurricular activities, most states have great resources to fit a variety of desires. Ask questions that relate to your family's interests and ages. If you have a teenager, inquire about teen groups. If you have preschool or elementary children, ask about play dates or art classes.

Will you ever figure out all the emotions and feelings of your children since your family moved? Well, we can sure try! Let's move on to the next chapter and "feel" our way through it!

Moving Closer Together

1. Ask your children how they would like you to be involved in their school.
2. Gather the supplies needed for a school scrapbook. As a project together, get the pages ready for all the fun things and memories of their first year in a new school.
3. During a family meal, go around the table and ask each person what the best thing was about his or her day at school.

4. Ask for specific prayer requests regarding school. Pray for one another.

5. Ask your children what areas in school they are struggling with the most. Encourage them with Ephesians 3:20, Philippians 1:6, Psalm 55:22, and Proverbs 16:3.

6. Share a memory you have of being the new kid at school when you moved as a child.

CHAPTER ELEVEN

Will I Feel Like This Forever? Dealing with the Emotions of Moving

The pain of leaving the place on which I had built
hopes and dreams for the future seemed unbearable.
I was filled with an attitude of anger and resentment.

ELIZABETH, AGE 15

Anger . . . I don't want to move!
  Sadness . . . leaving friends and school
    Fear . . . of the unknown
      Grief . . . over all the losses
        Loneliness . . . Nobody knows me.

Moving can be a traumatic emotional experience for all of us. It can cause our emotions to be like waves that swell in the ocean, then hit the beach with different degrees of force and flatten out, only to come back again with greater intensity. Our sea of emotions during the moving process can leave us feeling angry, sad, fearful, disappointed, hurt, resentful, anxious, and even depressed. The loss of identity and loneliness that follow after we move can hit us like an unexpected tidal wave, leaving us devastated. Although some people do sail smoothly through the moving process, for others it's like having the wind knocked out of their sails and then trying desperately to catch up with everybody else.

No one completely escapes the emotions of moving, but there always seems to be someone in the family who gets hit harder than others. At a time when you as a mom are trying to cope with your own emotions, you are also faced with the emotions of your children—especially your teenagers. Believe me, I know. It was all I could do to stay afloat emotionally myself. I was so overwhelmed when we moved that it was hard to even throw my children a life jacket. They had to somehow survive on their own.

Looking back, I know that turning to negativity and bitterness because of a move during adolescence is not the way to go. It was only damaging the people around me and myself, and was helpful to no one.

JEANNE, AGE 15

Perhaps going through this chapter will help you understand, and even validate, your own emotions, as well as recognize that your children could be going through similar feelings too. When we know we are all in the same boat, it's easier to work together and paddle in the same direction toward our destination.

You are still the main person who will be helping your children hands-on, one-on-one, and eye-to-eye with any moving issues. Will you let me encourage you as you sort through your own feelings during this chapter? Perhaps reading through these pages will force you to face any feelings you may have denied since you moved. Take some time to identify some of your reactions and then pray that God will begin the healing process in you. It is only then that you will be ready to come alongside your children as they deal with emotions they may not understand or have the coping skills to handle.

Grieving the Loss

Your family could be grieving right now over all that they left behind when they moved. It could be friends and extended family, or a home and a place they loved, your children's school, or a job. Leaving familiar people, places, and things to go to unfamiliar people, places, and things is not only a change and a disruption in our lives, but a great loss. We don't attach just our lives to people and places; we attach our hearts. That's what makes it so hard to move and that's why we grieve.

Do you know that grieving after a move is normal? (Do you even know that the word *normal* exists after a move?) There is no time frame for how long it will take each of you to go through the grieving process and begin to adjust to your new life. You will all feel a range of emotions at different times and you will all respond in different ways. Grieving is necessary. It helps you and your children adjust to the losses and change that come with the transition of moving.

Special Circumstances

The emotional losses of moving are compounded for children when there is the loss of a parent through divorce or the loss of a loved one through death. You and your family will first need to deal with the grief that comes with these life-changing situations before facing the losses in moving. With a divorce and then a move, children feel insecure and need the reassurance of both parents' love for them. They feel sad, and even angry, about the separation that comes with divorce and moving. They become fearful about the future and the safety of the absent parent. They could even feel responsible for the divorce, as well as the move.

To help ease their emotional losses, keep the lines of communication open for your children and the absent parent. Encourage visits, e-mails, letters, and phone calls. Even in a divorce situation, you can still work together for the emotional well-being of your child.

Moving can also be extremely stressful after the death of a loved one. If possible, it would be best not to move immediately after a death in the family. Each one of you will need a support system of friends and extended family as you work through the grieving process.

It will ease the pain of loss when you do move if you or your children do something in memory of your loved one. Consider a financial donation to your favorite charity or ministry in your loved one's name, or the symbol of planting flowers or a small tree in his or her memory. Your child might want to write a farewell letter, put it in a helium-filled balloon tied with a ribbon, and release it into the sky as a means of saying good-bye.

Other special circumstances are stressful and will make moving more difficult; for example, a major health issue, a tragedy that occurs, a financial crisis or bankruptcy, a custody situation, and even a sibling who moves away to college or stays behind. In all of these situations, your family will experience a sense of loss that makes moving more traumatic and the adjustment even harder.

Remember that everyone in the family will express their feelings of loss and grief differently. Emotions can be unpredictable during this time. As one 14-year-old put it, "I was overwhelmed with a feeling of indescribable sadness that made me feel weak." When you take a look at some of the emotions of moving, perhaps you will have better insight into how to love your children through these stressful situations in their lives.

Looking Deeper Within

Your children can go through various degrees of emotion after moving. Here are some of the reasons behind the feelings:

Anger—could be directed at the person or the circumstances they feel are responsible for the move, or because they feel they had no control over the decision.

Sadness—could be over having to leave everyone and everything, feeling the loss, and then longing for what will never be the same again.

Fear—could be from all the unknowns: Will everyone think I'm different because I'm new? Will I make friends? Will I like school? Will anyone speak to me, or will I be left out?

Disappointment—could come from things such as their school, friendships, house, or neighborhood being different from the way they had thought they would be (or the way they were before).

Resentment—could be from all the changes that are happening so fast; some are good, some are not so good.

Hurt—could be from the pain of separation and being disconnected from everybody and everything they left behind.

Anxiety—could be from worrying about any number of things: how they will begin to fit in at this new place; if they will make it in their new school academically, athletically, and socially; if they can find their way around the town; or even whether Mom or other family members are adjusting to the move.

Discuss the reasons behind the emotions with your children, so they will better understand why they feel the way they do. Ask them how they are feeling and share your own feelings. This is a great time to open a dialogue about everyone's reactions to moving.

Step by Step

Now that we've identified some of the emotions your child might have about moving, what do you do next? Christian counselor Patrick Middleton, who moved 29 times as a child, told me in an e-mail, "The problem is not the move; the problem is not helping kids to process the move. Parents aren't always skilled in how to help their kids, and they are absorbed in their own moving transition. They usually leave the kids alone to figure out this difficult experience. This robs kids of the opportunity to develop relational and coping skills they can use later in life."

So how do you help your children process their move? There are some key things you will want to remember that will help to pave the way:

- Get in the trenches with your kids. Share some of the feelings you had when you moved as a child. This lets them know they are not alone in their feelings.
- Provide an atmosphere of safety and freedom to express feelings openly.
- Give them permission to feel angry or sad. "You're not giving them permission to be disrespectful or destructive; but to feel what they're feeling. All emotions are acceptable, but all behaviors are not," writes David Ferguson in his book *Parenting with Intimacy*.[1]
- Children need to feel understood and supported when they express their feelings.
- Don't judge or criticize them when they express their emotions.
- Remind your children that their feelings are normal. Explain to them that grieving is part of the healing process after a move.
- Give them unconditional love and acceptance.
- Listen, listen, listen—with your heart, with your eyes, and in between the lines of conversation.
- Reassure them that it's okay to cry. Let the tears flow. They can be healing and cleansing for emotions.
- Keep communication open by encouraging everyone to talk during times of emotional stress points. Work at getting it all out on the table to better understand who, what, and why.
- Comfort your child. It can restore and soothe the emotions.
- Don't forget the value of touch. A hug can speak a thousand words. Holding your child in your arms can break down emotional walls.

• Remember, your children are watching how you respond to the situation. For the most part, they will take your lead emotionally.

Coauthor Thomas Olkowski says in his book *Moving with Children,* "Your task is simply to allow your children the opportunity to express their feelings openly without having to justify or defend them. This will allow them to adjust to the move at their own personal pace and, later, begin to evaluate it in a more positive light."[2]

Beyond the Surface

Watching for behavior that will reflect your child's feelings is a major way to determine that there is something going on beyond what the eye can see. Any behavior that is unusual or inconsistent with his or her normal behavior is a sign that your child could be struggling with the move. Following are some of the clues that might help you pinpoint the feelings or emotions behind the behavior:

Withdrawal

Loss of interest in school or grades that drop

Loss of interest in activities

Behaving badly

Prolonged crying or whining

Doesn't want to be separated from the family

Unusually fearful

Can't sleep or has nightmares

Outbursts for no obvious reason

A constant negative and complaining manner

Immature behavior

As you are sorting all this out, probably over a period of time, I want you to remember that you and your family will get through this. God is faithful and will not forsake you in your time of need. Kids are resilient and will bounce back, and you will become stronger through it all. Just remember to provide a lot of grace, and don't let a temporary feeling turn into a permanent relationship issue. Working through the emotions of moving is never easy, but it's worth the effort. Be sure your kids know that you care enough to reach into their world, not just as a parent, but as one who wants to understand the pain and provide comfort—just as Jesus does for us.

Extra Emotional Support—Provided by God's Word

For loneliness—"And lo, I am with you always" (Matthew 28:20).

For fear—"For God has not given us a spirit of timidity [fear], but of power and love and discipline [sound judgment]" (2 Timothy 1:7).

For anger—"Be angry, and yet do not sin; do not let the sun go down on your anger" (Ephesians 4:26).

For disappointment—"Trust in Him at all times, O people; pour out your heart before Him; God is a refuge for us" (Psalm 62:8).

For grief—"When you pass through the waters, I will be with you" (Isaiah 43:2).

For anxiety—"Cast your cares on the LORD and he will sustain you" (Psalm 55:22, NIV).

For sadness—"Weeping may remain for a night, but rejoicing comes in the morning" (Psalm 30:5, NIV).

For resentment—"I will give you a new heart and put a new spirit in you" (Ezekiel 36:26, NIV).

For hurt—"And the God of all grace, who called you to his eternal glory in Christ, after you have suffered a little while, will himself restore you and make you strong, firm and steadfast" (1 Peter 5:10, NIV).

For self-esteem—"For I am confident of this very thing, that He who began a good work in you will perfect it until the day of Christ Jesus" (Philippians 1:6).

For comfort—"Blessed are those who mourn, for they shall be comforted" (Matthew 5:4).

For hope—"This hope we have as an anchor of the soul, a hope both sure and steadfast" (Hebrews 6:19).

After reading this chapter, you probably feel like "lightening your load" is a great idea! You don't want to miss the next several pages. We're off the kids and on to you!

Moving Closer Together

1. Have everyone talk about who they miss the most, and what place or activity they miss the most since moving. How are you grieving for the loss? (Sadness, tears . . .) Comfort one another.
2. Which feeling(s) are you dealing with since the move? Why? Which step(s) will you take to help process those feelings? Pray for one another.
3. Now that feelings are shared, what are some specific ways each of you can encourage one another during the week? Encourage one another now.
4. Share what you have learned about your own feelings.
5. Tell which scripture(s) listed in the chapter comforts you the most. Look up other verses that apply to those feelings. Write down and memorize your favorites.
6. Talk about how Jesus comforts people and how He comforts you.

CHAPTER TWELVE

Lighten Your Load:
Hope and Encouragement
for Moms on the Move

God never says "forward" to His people without leading the way.[1]

Since you have taken the time to read this book and let me visit with you through its pages, you deserve a treat! Why don't we go outside and sit together for a while in my hammock. (Oh, come on, you can do it— just close your eyes and pretend.) It will be a nice break for you, and if you've never been in a hammock, you'll just love it. We might swing back and forth, or I will let you just rest there to refresh your body and mind.

One of the many reasons I love my hammock is that when I lie down and stretch out in it, I'm looking up at the sky. Looking up always helps me to keep my perspective on life. All my worries seem so small against the magnificence of the sky, and I can actually feel the sunshine (better known as the Sonshine!) on my face. So, let's just relax and enjoy these moments together. You can safely share your life and heart with me, and I will tell you some stories of women like you who have moved. When we part company soon, I want you to feel a new hope in your spirit and encouragement in your heart. In the course of our conversation, I want you to move again for me. No, I don't want you to get out of my hammock and leave! Listen to me first. My friend, I want you to move

> to a place of Trust
> to a place of Confidence
> to a place of Acceptance
> to a place of Contentment
> to a place of Peace
> to a place of Gratitude.

Then I will know you have arrived at the right place and you will be okay. Let's go to each of these places and linger a while.

Moving to a Place of Trust

Kim wrote me a letter to tell me the news. Her husband was with a large company and they were being transferred to another country. She had never moved out of the city limits and now she was moving halfway around the world. Kim was excited about the opportunity, but anxious about all the unknowns that faced her family. She was leaving a job she loved, her extended family, and a town where everybody knew her name.

As Kim described her feelings of sadness about leaving so much behind, I noticed how she kept coming back to the word *trust*. "I trust God in all of this," she wrote. "I'm anxious about the housing there, the kids' school, the language barrier—but, I trust God to work out the details. He's been faithful to us in the past, so I trust Him for our future."

I couldn't help but sense her calm spirit and inner strength through her words on each page. I knew, even with the adjustments ahead, she would be okay. She had already chosen to move to a place of trust in God. "Never be afraid to trust an unknown future to a known God," said Corrie ten Boom.[2]

How about you? Are you afraid to trust your unknown future to God? At a time when everything around you is changing, put your trust in an unchanging God who will not fail you or leave you, and who even prepares a place for you. He is the same yesterday, today, and tomorrow. You can depend on it. "In God I have put my trust; I shall not be afraid" (Psalm 56:4). "But as for me, I trust in You, O LORD. . . . My times are in Your hand" (Psalm 31:14-15).

Moving to a Place of Confidence

Trusting God with all your heart moves you to a place of confidence in Him. This is a confidence that says you are trusting in His will and plan for you and your family. "Such confidence we have through Christ" (2 Corinthians 3:4). Just as light shining through a prism is magnified and touches everything around a room, God's light shines through you and touches everything around you. Look for God's touch everywhere in your life.

"Look at how God worked through our move!" Laurie said with excitement. Surely this could not be the same Laurie who was in tears when they moved here a year before. Her daughter had just been diagnosed with a serious illness prior to their arrival. The stress of the illness, along with leaving her support system behind when they moved, had been almost too much for Laurie to handle emotionally and physically.

"At the time we didn't know that a doctor who specializes in Ashley's disease was right here in Phoenix," she said. "We kept looking for God in our move. We knew there had to be a reason we came here. We just couldn't see it at the time." I listened as she shared all about Ashley's life-changing medical care. Even through traumatic circumstances and confusion, Laurie had still looked for God in her family's move. She knew that "God causes all things to work together for good to those who love God, to those who are called according to His purpose" (Romans 8:28), and even though she couldn't see it at the time, God was working in their lives. Laurie had chosen to move to a place of confidence in God: "Therefore let us draw near with confidence . . . that we may receive mercy and find grace to help in time of need" (Hebrews 4:16).

Moving to a Place of Acceptance

Once you move to a place of confidence in God's plan and will for your life, then you can move to a place of acceptance. It is easier to accept your circumstances when your total trust and confidence are in God and not in what is happening in your life at the time: "For the things which are seen are temporal, but the things which are not seen are eternal" (2 Corinthians 4:18).

You begin by going back to Jesus.

I could tell by the look in her eyes that all was not good in her life. She smiled through the visible pain on her face and spoke quietly. "We moved here two weeks ago," she said softly. "My husband lost his job, and then we lost our house. We came here with our four children looking for a new beginning and a new job." She went on to say how they were living in an apartment with only what they could bring with them in a rented trailer.

I was expecting her at any minute to spiral downward into self-pity, but what she said was a testimony to me of a woman who had been moved, but not shaken. "I know God will use these circumstances in our lives to bring us closer to Him. We may have lost everything, but we haven't lost Jesus! Can I tell you what I've learned through this experience?" she said as she smiled. My heart was blessed as I listened to her tell about God's faithfulness and provision for them over the past few weeks.

Oswald Chambers says, "If God has made your cup sweet, drink it with grace; if He has made it bitter, drink it in communion with Him."[3] This young mom with four children is certainly drinking from her cup in communion with Him. She has chosen to accept her circumstances and make bitter become better. She is a woman who has chosen to move to a place of acceptance in her life.

Moving to a Place of Contentment

Once you have reached the place of acceptance, you are then ready to move to a place of contentment in your heart. Contentment truly is a state of the heart and has nothing to do with the state we live in.

Nothing had gone right for Cindy's family since they had moved three months before. They were living out of suitcases at the home of her in-laws while waiting for their new house to be built. Major construction problems meant they would be there another one to two months. The carpet had arrived in the wrong color, and the wallpaper had been lost in shipping. There seemed to be a new crisis with the house every day.

When her husband said, "Are we having fun yet?" it seemed to break the ice, and Cindy began to laugh. Her focus shifted from everything that was going wrong to all the things that were going right and what really mattered in her life. *It's okay,* she thought. *Regardless of what's going on around me, it's really okay. It may not be my way or my timing, but God will work it all out in His timing.*

She had come to a point of releasing her anxious concerns over the house and accepting the circumstances with peace of mind. Cindy had chosen to move to a place of contentment: "I have learned to be content in whatever circumstances I am" (Philippians 4:11). "The beauty of the house is order; the blessing of the house is contentment; the glory of the house is hospitality; the crown of the house is godliness."[4]

Moving to a Place of Peace

Once you've reached the place of contentment in your heart, you can then move next door to a place of peace. An inner peace comes from trusting God in all things, having confidence in His plan, accepting your circumstances, and feeling contentment in your heart regardless of your situation. Someone once said, "The peace of God is not the absence of problems; it is the presence of divine sufficiency in the midst of problems."

I saw an example of that not long ago. I watched Nell from across the room and marveled at the fact that she had even made it to our newcomers' event. She radiated warmth for others and a joyful spirit, and her smile lit up the room.

No one would have guessed the pain in her life. As a single mom, Nell and her two children moved to Phoenix from Texas. After 25 years of marriage, her husband had left her and the children. She was trying to start a new life in a new place. Her two teenagers were having a rough time adjusting to both their father's leaving and their move. One of them had run away from home, and Nell hadn't heard from him in two weeks.

Although her heart was heavy and sadness permeated her world, Nell reflected an inner peace that can come only from a close relationship with Jesus Christ. As I watched her, it was obvious she had moved to a place of peace in her life: "And the peace of God, which surpasses all comprehension, will guard your hearts and your minds in Christ Jesus" (Philippians 4:7).

Moving to a Place of Gratitude

Gratitude is the place everyone should move to! It is good to thank the Lord for every day He gives you. As the day begins, you can look ahead in faith and thank Him for His loving-kindness. As the day ends, you can look back and thank Him for His faithfulness: "I will give thanks to You, O Lord my God, with all my heart, and will glorify Your name forever. For Your lovingkindness toward me is great" (Psalm 86:12-13).

Robin didn't feel very grateful when she moved. In fact, she was so angry at her husband she couldn't feel anything. The wall between them was getting higher as they argued more and talked less. "Why did he do this to me?" she cried. "I left behind friends, my dream house, and a church I loved." Months went by and Robin's heart was still hardened by the move.

One day I got a phone call from her asking if she could come over for a few minutes. When I opened the door, she almost fell into my arms. "What am I going to do?" she said in desperation. "I'm a mess, my marriage is a mess—where do I begin?"

"You go back to Jesus; that's where you begin," I said. "He can heal your pain and restore your marriage. If you live in the midst of your mess for His glory, He'll work out the mess."

As the afternoon went by, we talked about all the things Robin had to be grateful for in her life since they had moved. Her husband loved her dearly, her kids were adjusting well, and she had gotten involved in a church Bible study and had made some friends. She began to see all the blessings in her life instead of all her unhappiness. As we prayed together before she left, I felt like a dark cloud had been lifted from Robin. I could see hope in her eyes. Yes, she and her husband had issues to work on in their marriage, but they were both willing to do whatever it would take to tear down the walls between them. They began with grateful hearts.

Don't let the things that aren't good about this move rob you of all the things that are good. Don't wait to feel grateful. Make the choice to be grateful. Remember that the feeling of gratefulness will follow the choice to be grateful. Gratitude will bring you back to Jesus. Go back to Him and thank Him for all your blessings. Start from there and then move forward.

I hope you've enjoyed our hammock time together. I pray that you are encouraged and leave with hope in your heart. More than that, I hope you leave knowing that you are not alone. God is there with you right now, and will never leave you. Trust Him with all your heart. He will give you far more than will ever be taken away from you in this move.

And remember, there are women just like you who move all over the world. They deal with the same feelings and frustrations. They worry about their kids. They get angry at their husbands. They hunger for a good friend. Many of them struggle with being a single parent, and they still haven't unpacked that last box. You, my friend, are not alone.

Fun and Frivolous Things to Do to Lighten Your Load (If You Don't Have a Hammock)

Go to a park and swing on the swings.

Go barefoot in the grass and wiggle your toes.

Go outside when it rains, look up, and let it rain on your face.

Buy yourself some fresh flowers and put them where you will enjoy them the most.

Rent a great "chick flick," fix some popcorn, prop your feet up— and enjoy with no guilt!

Visit a shop or a store that you've always wanted to go to, but never took the time to stop and browse.

Go outside, stand in the middle of your yard, look up, raise your arms, and say, "Thank You, God!" (It's not frivolous, but it does help lighten your load.)

What better gift to give your children than the gift of prayer. In the next chapter, we'll join hands as we pray for your children during this time of transition in their lives.

Moving Closer Together

1. Share what trusting God means to each family member. What is keeping one or more from moving to a place of trust in this move?
2. How has your confidence been shaken? Dwell in God's Word to help you move to a place of confidence.
3. What is the hardest thing to accept about this move? How will trusting God and putting your confidence in Him help you move to a place of acceptance in your life?
4. Are you living in a state of discontentment? Discuss how changing your focus can move you to a place of contentment.
5. What is robbing you of an inner peace about this move? Surrender each thing to God through prayer. Pray specifically for God to renew your mind as you begin to move to a place of peace in your heart.
6. List all the things you have to be grateful for at this season of your life. Move to a place of gratitude each day.

CHAPTER THIRTEEN

Now I Lay Me Down to Sleep: Praying for Your Children

On the day I found out we were moving I started praying
for our children's transition and adjustment.

A MOM ON THE MOVE

We had gathered together in Carla's living room to say our good-byes. She and her family were moving to California the following week, and the movers were expected to arrive any minute. As we sat in a circle to hear about their moving plans, I said, "How can we pray for you?" She sat there for a few seconds without saying anything, then looked around at everyone and said with a tender smile and tears in her eyes, "Pray for my girls. Pray they will make friends. Pray they will adjust to school. Just pray for my girls. That's how you can pray for me."

Since that day, I have often thought of how Carla's words reflect the heart of so many moms who move. No one can tug at our heartstrings like our children. As moms, we want to be a buffer between our children and the world. We want to protect them and soften the blow from any of the hard knocks of life, like moving.

One of the best ways I know to be a buffer for your children in this move, or anytime in their lives, is to pray for them: "Pour out your heart like water in the presence of the Lord. Lift up your hands to him for the lives of your children" (Lamentations 2:19, NIV). E. M. Bounds writes in his book *The Possibilities of Prayer,*

> Prayer blesses all things, brings all things, relieves all things and prevents all things. Everything as well as every place and every hour is to be ordered by prayer. Prayer has in it the possibility to affect everything that affects us.[1]

As a mom on the move, you probably would welcome some practical tips on prayer. First, we'll take a look at what prayer is, think about some ways to get started, and then decide how you can pray effectively for your children. The most important thing is that prayer becomes a part of who you are and a part of your life every day. "Prayer should be the key of the morning and the lock of the night."[2]

What's Prayer All About?

In *The Power of a Praying Parent,* Stormie Omartian writes, "Prayer is acknowledging and experiencing the presence of God and inviting His presence into our lives and circumstances. It's seeking the presence of God and releasing the power of God which gives us the means to overcome any problem."[3] She goes on to say that prayer is being in partnership with God as He shoulders the heaviness of the burden and provides wisdom, power, protection, and ability far beyond ourselves.

Many times I felt so overwhelmed with worry over Bill and Ginger. As my faith in God deepened, I began to release both of our children more and more to Him. As my trust in God increased, I became completely dependent on Him through prayer, rather than relying on myself to handle everything. Time spent with God in prayer began to deepen my relationship with Him, and my prayers began to change me, as well as the lives of our children.

I have discovered over the years that without the presence and power of God, I am totally inadequate and cannot make a difference in the lives of my children. A gentle reminder of what you may already know:

Prayer comes from the heart.

Prayer is like a personal conversation and is simply talking to God and with God.

You can either pray aloud or pray silently. You can pray anywhere and anytime.

There is no technique to praying; the best way to begin is just to start talking to God!

Scriptures to Encourage Your Prayer Time

Being in God's Word will not only be an encouragement to your heart, it will be the foundation of your prayer time. As you spend time with God through His Word and in prayer, your relationship and knowledge of Him will deepen. These are some of my favorite prayer verses from the Bible. Take a moment to meditate on each one.

"The effective prayer of a righteous man can accomplish much" (James 5:16).

"In the morning, O LORD, You will hear my voice; in the morning I will order my prayer to You and eagerly watch" (Psalm 5:3).

"Pray without ceasing" (1 Thessalonians 5:17).

"Be anxious for nothing, but in everything by prayer and supplication with thanksgiving let your requests be made known to God" (Philippians 4:6).

"Devote yourselves to prayer, keeping alert in it with an attitude of thanksgiving" (Colossians 4:2).

"Draw near to God and He will draw near to you" (James 4:8).

"Cast all your anxiety on him because he cares for you" (1 Peter 5:7, NIV).

"At all times they ought to pray and not to lose heart" (Luke 18:1).

"So I have also dedicated him to the LORD; as long as he lives he is dedicated to the LORD" (1 Samuel 1:28).

Getting Down to the Details

A good way to begin your prayer time is by making a list of every concern and every detail of your child's life that you want to cover in prayer. God cares about every intricate detail of our lives. Nothing in life is too small or too big to take to Him in prayer. You can use a spiral notebook as a prayer journal, or write a list of prayer needs on paper to insert in your Bible or in your appointment calendar for easy reference.

Then ask God specifically how to pray for your child. Ask Him for wisdom, clarity, and direction in praying. You will be amazed at the things He will reveal to you when you ask.

I encourage you to pray Scripture over your child and claim God's promises through His Word. Write specific Bible verses for each child in your prayer notes or by their name in your prayer journal. Though my kids are grown now, I still love to feel that I am connecting my children to God through His Word. In the front of their Bibles, you might want to write a special prayer for each of your children as an encouragement to them. What a treasure that prayer will be for years to come.

When I pray for my children and grandchildren, there are several basic elements I like to include. As I begin to pray, I focus on God as I praise Him for who He is and tell Him how much I love Him. I want to pray with a pure heart, so I ask His forgiveness for anything wrong I may have said or done. Next, I express my gratitude to God for all His blessings in my life. Lastly, I humbly make my prayer requests known to

God. This has become a natural process of my prayer life when I pray for others.

A prayer basket keeps everything close at hand and is a must for praying moms. In my basket is a Bible, my prayer notebook, a pen, some 3 x 5 cards, Post-it notes, and a picture of my family. When my kids were still at home, I loved to write on a Post-it, "I'm praying for you today!" or "I've got you covered in prayer!" and stick it in school notebooks or in the kids' rooms.

I also keep a picture of our children and grandchildren in the front of my appointment calendar as a visual reminder to pray for them. Some moms on the move put Post-it notes or 3 x 5 cards in their cars or around the house as prayer reminders. Don't forget, too, that Moms in Touch International is a great way to connect with other moms who are praying for their kids. Find the best means with which to deepen and enrich your prayer life for your children and go for it!

For Busy Moms on the Run

Wherever you are and whatever you're doing, you can always pray for your children. When you are on the run, try these:

When you're in the car, pray at stoplights.

Pray when you are waiting in line after school to pick up your children.

Pray when you are carpooling (pray for the other children as well) or waiting to pick up your kids from an activity.

When you're jogging or walking, exercise your thoughts toward prayer!

When you are standing in that long line at the checkout counter, instead of flipping through a magazine, try praying!

When your call is put on hold, take advantage of the moment to send up a prayer.

When you're waiting for an appointment, that prayer list in your appointment calendar can be real handy.

You will identify with this poem as a busy mom on the move. It will prod you to pray!

A.S.A.P.
(Always Say A Prayer)

There's work to do, deadlines to meet,
you've got no time to spare,
But as you hurry and scurry,
Always Say A Prayer.

In the midst of family chaos,
"quality time" is rare.
Do your best; let God do the rest:
Always Say A Prayer.

It may seem like your worries
are more than you can bear.
Slow down and take a breather—
Always Say A Prayer.

God knows how stressful life is;
He wants to ease our cares,
And He'll respond **A.S.A.P.**—
Always Say A Prayer.[4]

—Lisa O. Engelhardt

Before We Say Good-Bye

I've shared many practical ideas in this book to help your children through the moving process. However, these are the things of greatest value that I want you to treasure in your heart and give to your children:

Prayer. Let them see you pray, hear you pray, and watch you give God the credit for the results. (Philippians 4:6)

Principles of faith. Base your values on the Word of God. (Colossians 2:6-7)

Pattern of life. Strive to live a life worthy of imitation that models God's design. (Ephesians 5:1-2)

Persistence that is immovable. Don't give up. Don't let anything move you from what you believe. Be strong in your faith. (Ephesians 6:10, 14)

Participation. Feel what your children feel. Laugh when they laugh. Cry when they cry. Learn with them. (Romans 12:15)

Praise. Encourage them. Believe in them. Sing to them when they are small. Sing with them when they are grown. (Ephesians 5:19-20)

Planning. It's never too late. Plan on giving them "roots" in Jesus and "wings" to soar to their potential![5] (Isaiah 40:31)

A Great Beginning . . .

What a great way to end our time together—by beginning with prayer! As you begin to pray for your children and meet Jesus face-to-face, He won't say to you, "You didn't get all those boxes unpacked yet," or "You didn't get everything done on your list today." What He would say is, "You took time to pray today . . . you put your children first . . . you gave them a hug . . . you listened."

The choice is yours. You decide what is important and what has the greatest impact on your children. You don't have to have life all together to pray; you just have to love your kids enough to put them in God's hands.

. . . Always Comes to an End

There are always so many things to share when friends are drawn together by a common bond, and saying good-bye is never easy. Our bond as "friends in Christ" and "moms who move" will always connect us heart to heart. Perhaps one day we can catch up on some more special time together, and you can swing in my hammock to your heart's content. I will look forward to your knock on my door.

Remember that I believe in you. I'm standing on the sidelines, waving my pom-poms and cheering you on. You can make it, and so can your children!

Your biggest fan,
Susan

P.S. Remember to "go back to Jesus" and start from there!

Appendix 1
Prayers from Moms Who Move

To guide you in praying effectively, I've included some prayers from moms who move. Consider using one or more of these prayers to pray for your children during this time of transition. Personalize the prayer you choose by inserting your child's name and including your child's own specific needs.

———

O Lord, restore my children's hearts. Heal any hurts that may have come from all the times we've moved. Lord, remove from their hearts any bitterness or anger they might feel, and replace those feeling with good memories from all our moves. I pray You would bring forgiveness to their hearts for all of the mistakes we made as parents during the times we moved and were insensitive to their needs.

When they look back, may they see that the things You taught them through moving are things they couldn't have learned any other way. Thank You, Lord, that not only do You work in the present and prepare the future, but You also heal the past. In Jesus' name, Amen.

———

I come to You again, dear Lord, on bended knee. I am overwhelmed by my own sense of grief at what we left behind when we moved. Father, my heart is broken for our children. They also miss everything and everybody we left behind when we moved. I know Your Word teaches that You work all things out for our good, but our children are suffering through this move.

May I be a cup of encouragement to them today. Help me to minister to them in a way that would soothe their hurt. Equip me to understand their hearts and know when to be quiet and listen, when to speak up and instruct, and when to encourage or correct them. Please, Lord, let someone be kind to them today at school. Be a Friend to each of them, Lord. May they feel Your presence throughout the day. In the name of Jesus, I come to You. Amen.

Dear Lord,

Please guide and protect our children as they start the first day of school in a new place. Surround them with your angels and help them to not be afraid. Lead them to Christian friends. Please let someone sit with them at lunch and play with them on the playground. Give their teachers an extra measure of patience, kindness, and sensitivity since they are new to school. I pray this will be a good year for them, and that they will walk closely with You. In Jesus' name, Amen.

Father God,

Thank You for who You are. Thank You for allowing this wonderful opportunity to stretch us as we move. I ask for Your guidance as I try to be an example for my children during the transition of moving. I pray for patience and a willing spirit that can come only from You. Through my example, I pray that my children will look to You for their security. I pray they will understand that You have a plan for their lives that includes this move.

Please protect them, and guide them toward new friends and activities that will glorify You. I'm reminded of the many times that I've looked back at our moves and always seen Your hand in the situation. You continue to bless us through these difficult times.

I ask for all this in the name of Your precious Son Jesus, Amen.

———

Heavenly Father,

Thank You that You care about all the details of my family's life. Thank You that You gave us peace and direction in this move. Lord, I thank You for Your promise that You will be with us, that You will never leave or forsake us. Your Word says to be strong and courageous, to not be terrified, to not be discouraged. Thank You for the assurance of Your Word.

I lift up my children to You. I pray a hedge of protection around them. I pray that they will be drawn to new friends who know You. I pray that they will not be attracted to evil and will not be led into temptation. I pray that they will stay on Your straight path and not swerve to the right or the left. I pray that they won't give in to peer pressure, but that they will see themselves through Your eyes as a child of God, valued and loved.

I thank You for the plans that You have for their lives—plans to prosper them and not to harm them, plans to give them a hope and a future. I pray that they will catch a vision of the purpose You have for their lives.

Help me as a mom to keep Your Word in my heart and my eyes on You and not on my circumstances. I thank You that You have Your hand on all of us. In Jesus' name, Amen.

———

Dear Lord,

You know the weight on my heart for my children. Give me the wisdom to guide and direct them through every aspect of this move. Give me the discernment to know if they're hiding or stuffing their fears and hurts. Give me the grace not to wrongly react to any anger or frustration. Give me the words of truth to ease their anxieties. Give me the sensitivity to calmly and quietly listen and to clearly understand what they are going through.

Give me the strength not to weigh them down with my own hurts and concerns. Give me the courage not to sweep anything under the rug, or to blow anything out of proportion. Give me inner peace as I stand on Your promises and trust that You are with my children every step of the way. In Jesus' name I pray, Amen.

~

Dear Lord,

Thank You for these precious children that You have given me. I pray that You will be a real part of their everyday lives. When they are scared or confused, I pray they will go to You first and ask for Your help, then come to me. Help them to be generous and kind to others and make friends easily. As they grow, give them a servant's heart to serve You in some way.

Let the family always be a safe place to come and share their problems and concerns. Help me to give wise answers to the hard questions. Help me to teach them right from wrong at an early age, and instill in them the love of Christ. May they come to know You and love You with their whole hearts, and follow You all the days of their lives. In Jesus' precious name, Amen.

~

Dear Lord,

I pray for our children—that You would be their rock and their shield in this move. I pray they would turn to You to meet their needs, and not to the first friendly face. Protect them from evildoers. I pray they would be friendly to everyone but discerning in whom they choose for friends. Let them not succumb to peer pressure, but be able to find great Christian friends that will last a lifetime. I pray that they would not get into the wrong crowd, and that Your Holy Spirit would direct their every step.

Help me to keep my mouth shut and not to constantly nag about things of little importance. I need to choose my battles wisely and fight only the ones that really matter for eternity. Give me strength to let go of mothering (smothering) and give them room to grow to be the children that You designed them to be. I give my children up to You and know that Your plan for their lives is better than any plan I could devise. In Jesus' name, Amen.

Dear Heavenly Father,

Thank You, Lord, for these wonderful children You have given to us. I pray, Lord, that You will keep them very near and dear to You as they start going to a new school. I pray for protection as they move about the campus. I pray they will make wise choices in the friends they choose. I pray they will have wisdom to discern when they are in an unhealthy situation, and that You will give them the strength and courage to walk away from those situations. Lord, help them to recognize their gifts and talents from You, and to find places where they can use them. I pray they will choose to study hard and be brave when they need to ask for help. Surround them with Your love, Lord, and let them know how much we love and care for them. Amen.

⌣

Dear Lord,

I thank You for the very life of my children and the joy of their presence. Through them, You have allowed me to understand unconditional love. As we move, Lord, help them to recognize the difference between what is worldly and what is godly. Guard and protect their thoughts and their hearts. May Your presence surround them, and may You always hold them close. May they learn in the days ahead to turn to You in times of need. Thank You, Lord, that You have given them a spirit of joy. Thank You for all the joy they bring to our family. With a grateful heart, Amen.

Appendix 2
Letters to God from Kids Who Move

I could feel the heartbeat of kids who move as I read through their letters to God. You will get a closer look at moving from their perspective as you read excerpts from some of their letters. It might even help you better understand your own kids' thoughts about moving. You will catch a glimpse of their humor and their sadness, their victories and their defeats, their joy and their pain. (These letters are unedited to preserve the original spelling and punctuation.)

Dear God,
I am very happy wherever you put me. I think my house is okay. I just don't like the stairs. I love my teachers and school a lot. So everything is fine.
Talk to you soon. Amber, age 10

Dear God,
Our cat did not like the long car ride to Texas. I like my new school. I have mad a lot of friends. We have not found a church yet but we are still looking.
I love you! Sierra, age seven

~

Dear God,

I hate moving becase we have to leave all are freindes behind. It was hard to make new freindes. When I moved I did not like it becase I missed my freindes. I missed ever buddie in the naberhood. Savannah, age six

~

Dear God,

I'm only eleven and I have lived in six different houses and four different schools. The hardest part of moving is leaving friends. Not just any friends, but friends who you've shared secrets with, and have become very close to. It seems really unfair to have to move just because of parents work. The first day at a new school is really scary and lonely, because you don't know anyone and it brings back memories of your old friends.

Love, Margaret, age 11

~

Dear God,

Most families don't move around like my family has. This will be my 7th school in 11 years, and this move feels like the hardest one yet. The worst part is how lonely I feel. I am dreading having to start all over again. I don't want to make my parents feel bad so I try to act like it is no big deal, but inside I am nervous and worried. Julie, age 15

~

Dear God,

Please let me go back. Zack, age 11

~

Dear God,

Why did you bring me here? It is so lonely here. I have no friends. I don't like my room. Please fix these problems and if that doesn't work I want to go back home! Megan, age nine

~

Dear God,

I know you care but I sure could use some more help. I am mad at Mom and Dad, mostly Dad for taking this job. I miss my friends. Please help me to like it here. Love, John, age 10

~

Dear God,

I would ask you to guide me so I not a lot scared. That's all. Carly, age six

~

Dear God,

It is so hard being the new kid. Thanks for listening. Riley, age nine

~

Dear God,

When you move it is cool that you end up with new friends. Adam, age eight

~

Dear God,

We read the Bible together and pray. But I am still lonely. Brian, age eight

———

Dear God,

We moved in with my grandpa until my mom and dad find the house they want. It was 2 years before we found a house. We did a lot of house hunting. Now I have my own room and my grandpa doesn't get in my hair about eating a healthy breakfast. Sarah, age eight

———

Dear God,

Please let the other kids like me. I will be nice at the same time. Please let me have nice teachers, and I will respect them. Love, Alix, age 10

———

Dear God,

When I was moving I was nuves about my new school and new friend and new home. Love, Emma, age seven

———

Dear God,

When I moved I missed my old friends but I got new friends. I missed my old house but I got a new house. Brett, age eight

———

Dear God,

Adjusting to a new school is nice because everyone pays attention to you but after a while it wears off. Love, Jennifer, age 15

~

Dear God,

When we moved I was mad, sad, and angry. My sister had no trouble with it but I did. Love, Jessica, age 13

~

Dear God,

At my good bye party at school people were hugging me and telling me how much I was going to be missed. I wanted to race home to tell my Dad I wasn't moving anywhere. Sincerely, Katie, age nine

~

Dear God,

The best thing about moving is that I got a new cat. Brenda, age six

~

Dear God,

Thank you for three bathrooms in our new house. Brianna, age nine

~

Dear God,

We moved cause my Mom thought our new house was cute and better. Savannah, age seven

Dear God,
I am trying to keep my head up high since we moved. Thomas, age 11

Dear God,
We have to move cause my dad got laid off and couldn't find a job. Please help him find a job. Mark, age seven

Dear God,
I wish my parents would look at things from my point of view a little more when we moved. Dottie, age 13

Appendix 3
Finding the Best School
for Your Child

Where Do You Start?

Since school will be the hub of your child's life, that's where we'll begin. If you haven't moved yet, hopefully you have already set the wheels in motion to find the best school for your children. The Internet is a great tool for research, as is the library. When possible, many families will select a school first and then the area or neighborhood where they will move.

First, Check It Out

These are some things you will want to consider as you inquire about a school in your new area:
- Curriculum. Find out what the school will be teaching. Ask about the basics that are covered. Inquire about electives and extracurricular activities, like sports or clubs.
- Policies. Ask about rules on discipline and homework. Ask for a copy of the student handbook and a school calendar for the year. How is school spirit built among the students?
- Facilities. Look for adequate classrooms, cafeteria, physical education facilities, playground, and an auditorium or large room for performances and meetings. Does the school accommodate children with special needs?

- Staff. Find out the student/teacher ratio. Inquire about the number of teachers on staff and their educational requirements. Ask if there are counselors and gifted or special education teachers on staff for any specific needs your child might have.
- Academic standards. Ask to see past test scores. How are students prepared for SATs? Your local education authority (LEA) produces a booklet that lists all the schools in your area with lots of information on each school. Also check out The School Report at www.homefair.com.
- If you have a child with special needs, contact the National Parent Network on Disabilities for a local chapter in your new area (1727 King Street, Suite 305, Alexandria, Va. 22314).
- If you homeschool your child, contact the National Home School Association for a group in your new area (P.O. Box 290, Hartland, Mich. 48353).

Note: Although many of the factors you would consider in a public or private school situation do not apply to homeschooling, the emotional and social adjustment needs that come with moving apply to any child.

Second, Scope It Out

Here are some hands-on things to do to help your children become more comfortable with their new school. It will also give them a sense of security and reduce anxiety.

- Register as soon as you can. Personally deliver copies of academic and immunization records.
- Make an appointment to meet with the principal and the teacher(s) before your child's first day.
- Tour the campus with your child. Scope out the key places they will go on the first day—the classroom, cafeteria, and bathrooms. Locate the office, the gym, the library, and the playground.

- If your child rides the bus, find out the bus number and where the school buses pick up and drop off students.
- If you drive your child to school, or if your teenager drives to school, find out the rules and where to park.
- Ask what your child will need to bring to school the first day.
- Ask about any additional costs for supplies or activities.

Finding Homeschool Groups

There is a worldwide organization for homeschooling called Home School Legal Defense Association. Their Web site, www.hslda.org, can link you to national and international homeschooling organizations and connect you to support groups in your new area. HSLDA will also inform you of the laws in the state to which you are moving.

Notes

Introduction

1. Kristin A. Hansen, *Geographical Mobility: March 1995 to March 1996*, U.S. Bureau of the Census, Current Population Reports, P20-473, U.S. Government Printing Office, Washington, D.C., 1997.

Chapter 4

1. Serenity Prayer, source and author unknown.
2. Leslie Levine, *Will This Place Ever Feel Like Home?* (New York: Contemporary Books, a division of McGraw-Hill, 2002), 218.

Chapter 5

1. George MacDonald, quoted in *A Celebration of You*, compiled by Larissa Nygren (Uhrichsville, Ohio: Barbour, 2002), 37.

Chapter 7

1. Audrey McCollum, M.S.W., Nadia Jensen, Ed.D., Stuart Copans, M.D., *Smart Moves* (Lyme, N.H.: Smith and Kraus Publishers, Inc., 1996), 127.
2. Stephen R. Covey, *The 7 Habits of Highly Effective Families* (New York: Golden Books, 1997), 216.

Chapter 8

1. John Trent, Ph.D., *Be There!* (Colorado Springs, Colo.: Water-Brook Press, 2000), 101.
2. Ibid., 111-12.

Chapter 9

1. Thomas T. Olkowski, Ph.D., and Lynn Parker, Ph.D., *Moving with Children* (Littleton, Colo.: Gylantic Publishing Co., 1993), 105-6.
2. Carolyn Janik, *Positive Moves* (New York: Weidenfeld and Nicolson, 1988), 147.
3. Neil Bernstein, quoted in "Friends for Life," by Caralee Adams, *Better Homes and Gardens* (August 2002): 84.

Chapter 10

1. Kristin A. Hansen. *Geographical Mobility: March 1995 to March 1996*, U.S. Bureau of the Census, Current Population Reports, P20-473, U.S. Government Printing Office, Washington, D.C., 1997.

Chapter 11

1. Dr. David and Teresa Ferguson, Dr. Paul and Vicky Warren, Terri Ferguson, *Parenting with Intimacy* (Colorado Springs, Colo.: Victor Books, 1995), 121.
2. Thomas T. Olkowski, Ph.D., and Lynn Parker, Ph.D., *Moving with Children* (Littleton, Colo.: Gylantic Publishing Co., 1993), 38.

Chapter 12

1. Author unknown, quote taken from personal study notes.
2. Corrie ten Boom, quoted by Warren Wiersbe in *With the Word* (Nashville: Oliver-Nelson Books, 1991), 278.
3. Oswald Chambers, *My Utmost for His Highest* (New York: Dodd, Mead, 1935), November 11 reading, 316.
4. An old motto often placed about fireplaces, author unknown. Quoted by Wiersbe in *With the Word,* 399.

Chapter 13

1. E. M. Bounds, *The Possibilities of Prayer* (Springdale, Pa.: Whitaker House, 1994), 87.
2. Author unknown, quoted in a "Prayer Leaflet" flyer.
3. Stormie Omartian, *The Power of a Praying Parent* (Eugene, Ore.: Harvest House, 1995), 18.
4. Lisa O. Engelhardt © Abbey Press, St. Meinrad, Ind., 1999. Used with permission.
5. The seven principles are taken from *After the Boxes are Unpacked,* by Susan Miller (Colorado Springs, Colo.: Focus on the Family, 1995). 118.

Resources

Organizations

Focus on the Family; Colorado Springs, CO 80995; 1-800-A-FAMILY (1-800-232-6459); www.family.org

Hearts at Home; 900 W. College, Normal, IL 61761; 1-309-888-MOMS; www.hearts-at-home.org

Moms in Touch International; P.O. Box 1120, Poway, CA 92074-1120; 1-800-949-MOMS; www.momsintouch.org

N.E.W. Ministries; P.O. Box 5692, Scottsdale, AZ 85261-5692; 1-480-991-5268; www.justmoved.org

Young Life; 420 N. Cascade, Colorado Springs, CO 80903; 1-719-381-1800; www.younglife.org

Internet Sites

www.artofmoving.com
www.mapquest.com
www.move.com
www.tckworld.com
www.single-parent.family.org

Publishers

BR Anchor Publishing; Wilmington, N.C.; www.branchor.com; a relocation information publishing house providing domestic and international books for adults, teenagers, preteens, and young children

Recommended Reading
and Viewing

Books

Preschool Age

Asch, Frank. *Goodbye House.* Englewood Cliffs, N.J.: Prentice Hall, 1986.

Berenstain, Stan and Jan. *The Berenstain Bears' Moving Day.* New York: Random House, 1981.

McGeorge, Constance. *Boomer's Big Day.* San Francisco: Chronicle Books, 1994.

Elementary Age

Davis, Gabriel. *The Moving Book: A Kids' Survival Guide.* Tigard, Ore.: First Books, 1997 and 2003.

Lowry, Lois. *Anastasia Again!* Boston: Houghton Mifflin, 1981.

Viorst, Judith. *Alexander, Who's Not (Do You Hear Me? I Mean It!) Going to Move.* New York: Atheneum Press, 1995.

Preteens and Teens

Freeman, Martha. *The Year My Parents Ruined My Life.* Holiday House, 1997. (Middle school)

Moms

Carlisle, Ellen. *Smooth Moves.* Charlotte, N.C.: Teacup Press, 1999.

Chapman, Gary. *The Five Love Languages: How to Express Heartfelt Commitment to Your Mate.* Chicago: Northfield Publishing, 1992.

Fuller, Cheri. *When Mothers Pray.* Sisters, Ore.: Multnomah Publishers, 1997.

Howe, Michele. *Going It Alone: Meeting the Challenges of Being a Single Mom.* Peabody, Mass.: Hendrickson Publishers, 2003.

Kay, Ellie. *Heroes at Home: Help and Hope for America's Military Families.* Bloomington, Minn.: Bethany House Publishers, 2002.

Levine, Leslie. *Will This Place Ever Feel Like Home?* New York: Contemporary Books, a division of McGraw-Hill, 2002.

McCollum, Audrey, M.S.W., Nadia Jensen, Ed.D., Stuart Copans, M.D. *Smart Moves.* Lyme, N.H.: Smith and Kraus Publishers, Inc., 1996.

Miller, Susan. *After the Boxes Are Unpacked: Moving On After Moving In.* Colorado Springs, Colo.: Focus on the Family, 1995.

Olkowski, Thomas T., Ph.D., and Lynn Parker, Ph.D., *Moving with Children.* Littleton, Colo.: Gylantic Publishing Co., 1993.

Omartian, Stormie. *The Power of a Praying Parent.* Eugene, Ore.: Harvest House Publishers, 1995.

Waddell, Marshele. *Hope for the Home Front: God's Timeless Encouragement for Today's Military Wife.* Virginia Beach, Va.: One Hope Ministry, 2003.

Video

Tucker, Karen and Murphy, Jane. "Let's Get a Move On!" Newton, Mass.: Kidvidz, 1990.

N.E.W. Ministries supports and encourages moms who move by offering classes and small groups that are held in churches, neighborhoods, military bases, seminaries, and companies that relocate families. (Check www.justmoved.org for a class in your area.) N.E.W. Ministries also offers books, videos, seminars, conferences, and newsletters to help moms through the adjustment and transition of moving. If you want to know more about N.E.W. Ministries and its outreach to women and their families, contact us at:

N.E.W. Ministries
P.O. Box 5692
Scottsdale, AZ 85261
1-480-991-5268
Web site: *www.justmoved.org*
E-mail: *newministries@justmoved.org*

I would love to hear from you! We welcome your comments, moving stories, and kids' moving tips. If you have recently moved or if you are moving and would like to receive our NEWcomer's Newsletter, e-mail us or sign up on the Web site!

FOCUS ON THE FAMILY®

Welcome to the Family!

Whether you received this book as a gift, borrowed it, or purchased it yourself, we're glad you read it. It's just one of the many helpful, insightful, and encouraging resources produced by Focus on the Family.

In fact, that's what Focus on the Family is all about—providing inspiration, information, and biblically based advice to people in all stages of life.

It began in 1977 with the vision of one man, Dr. James Dobson, a licensed psychologist and author of 18 best-selling books on marriage, parenting, and family. Alarmed by the societal, political, and economic pressures that were threatening the existence of the American family, Dr. Dobson founded Focus on the Family with one employee and a once-a-week radio broadcast aired on only 36 stations.

Now an international organization, the ministry is dedicated to preserving Judeo-Christian values and strengthening and encouraging families through the life-changing message of Jesus Christ. Focus ministries reach families worldwide through 10 separate radio broadcasts, two television news features, 13 publications, 18 Web sites, and a steady series of books and award-winning films and videos for people of all ages and interests.

• • •

For more information about the ministry, or if we can be of help to your family, simply write to Focus on the Family, Colorado Springs, CO 80995 or call (800) A-FAMILY (232-6459). Friends in Canada may write Focus on the Family, P.O. Box 9800, Stn. Terminal, Vancouver, B.C .V6B 4G3 or call (800) 661-9800. Visit our Web site—www.family.org—to learn more about Focus on the Family or to find out if there is an associate office in your country.

We'd love to hear from you!

Must-Have Books for Moms!

from Focus on the Family

After the Boxes Are Unpacked

Moving can be a heavy strain on a marriage, and a traumatic event in a woman's life. Susan Miller's advice reminds women they're not alone, and helps make their transition more smooth and less overwhelming. With ingenious insights and helpful hints, this great gift book makes relocation a real moving experience! Paperback.

Peacemaking for Families

Conflict is inevitable and perfectly normal. Learning how to handle it realistically and biblically is the key to peace. Using forgiveness, negotiation and listening techniques that have helped countless families reach a new appreciation of each other, the authors coach families into learning how to handle their feelings and manage their moods in a positive way. Paperback.

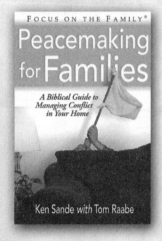

The Mom You're Meant to Be

Motherhood is meant to be a blessing, not a burden. So why do so many moms seem exhausted? Cheri Fuller's *The Mom You're Meant to Be* encourages mothers to relax, embrace their children's individuality and rely on God for the wisdom they need. Hardcover.

Look for these special books in your Christian bookstore or request a copy by calling (800) A-FAMILY. Friends in Canada may write to Focus on the Family, PO Box 9800, Stn Terminal, Vancouver, BC V6B 4G3 or call (800) 661-9800.